JUSTICE UNBALANCED

Gender, Psychiatry and Judicial Decisions

Hilary Allen

Open University Press

Milton Keynes · Philadelphia

129408

Open University Press
Open University Educational Enterprises Limited
12 Cofferidge Close
Stony Stratford
Milton Keynes MK11 1BY, England

and
242 Cherry Street
Philadelphia, PA 19106, USA

First published 1987

British Library Cataloguing in Publication Data

Allen, Hilary
    Justice unbalanced : gender, psychiatry
    and judicial decisions.
    1. Sex discrimination in criminal justice
    administration
    I. Title
    364.6′088042   HV6046

    ISBN 0–335–15521–9

    ISBN 0–335–15520–0 Pbk

Library of Congress Cataloging in Publication Data
Allen, Hilary (Hilary Mavis)
    Justice unbalanced.
    Bibliography: p.
    Includes index.
    1. Insanity — Jurisprudence — United States.
2. Sex discrimination in criminal justice administra-
tion — United States.   3. Female offenders — Legal
status, laws, etc. — United States.   I. Title.
KF9242.A83   1987   345.73′04   87–22088
                        347.3054
ISBN 0–335–15521–9
ISBN 0–335–15520–0 (pbk.)

Text design by Clarke Williams

Typeset by Marlborough Design
Printed in Great Britain at the Alden Press, Oxford

To Cheryl Fitzgerald

Contents

List of Figures

Acknowledgements

Many organizations and individuals have helped me in the course of this project. My apologies that so few of them are named individually here, but my thanks to them all.

Nikolas Rose supervised the thesis on which this book is based, and patiently guided it through innumerable drafts and reconstructions. His intelligence, criticism, kindness and sense of humour all lightened the difficulties of the study, and the experience of working with him added enormously to its pleasures.

The research was funded by a grant from the Economic and Social Research Council and was based in the Department of Human Sciences at Brunel University, where I was given much encouragement and practical help by the academic, secretarial and technical staff. My field-work took me to courts, hospitals and government offices, and there I received help from large numbers of officials and professional personnel, including doctors and hospital managers; magistrates, lawyers, and clerks of court; officers of the Metropolitan Police, the Prison Service and the Probation Service; and officials from the Home Office and the Lord Chancellor's Department. In their different ways, these various people all gave generously of both time and expertise. They patiently answered my questions, allowed me to watch them at work, and helped me to collect my empirical data. Additionally, I am indebted to Dr Joanna Shapland, who discussed sentencing with me, and gave me access to an invaluable collection of transcripts from magistrates' courts.

I also want to thank my friends for their support and patience throughout the years of this project. Cheryl Fitzgerald helped me to think about the crimes, the people, and the dilemmas of this field, adding a much-needed compassion to my severest thoughts about all of them. Joan Davis supported my work in countless ways, and her intelligent questions and genuine encouragement contributed far more than she realises to its completion. I am also grateful to David and Liz Freedman, Shafika Schlicht and Liz

Lockwood, all of whom gave me shelter during bad times of this study, and kept me in touch with a good world outside it.

Finally, I thank Cath Jackson, who not only illustrated the cover but also gave up much time to read and discuss with me the entire last draft of the book. Her interest and suggestions much eased this final transformation, and her felicitous editings have averted some terrible prose.

Introduction

A woman appearing before the criminal court is about twice as likely as a man to be dealt with by psychiatric rather than penal means. In the first place, psychiatric considerations are more likely to influence the verdict of the court: she is more likely than a man to be found unfit to plead or not guilty by reason of insanity, and in a case of homicide by a woman, the offence will more frequently be reduced to manslaughter on grounds of diminished responsibility. In the second place, if convicted of a crime, she is also more likely than a man to be ordered to receive psychiatric treatment instead of a normal penalty. This book examines the reasons for the sexual discrepancy in the use of such psychiatric measures by the courts.

It describes the findings of a research project which examined the reasoning behind these medical and judicial decisions. The study is a qualitative one, entailing the detailed analysis of a variety of medical and legal texts: the formal laws, statutes and precedents governing the involvement of psychiatry in the treatment of offenders; the policies for psychiatric provision and organization; medical and legal documents from a sample of male and female cases; recorded statements by various professional personnel; and transcripts from the courts.

In the course of the analysis, many of the seemingly obvious explanations for the discrepancy are necessarily rejected. The discrepancy cannot be accounted for by sexual differences in the mental health of male and female offenders, since there remains a sexual discrepancy in the pattern of disposal even if one looks at cases that are similarly diagnosed. Nor can the difference be explained by the assertion that the authorities view criminal men as 'bad' but criminal women as 'mad'. If anything, judicial personnel seem more conscious of the madness of their *male* offenders, and ironically enough it is often the apparent severity of their madness that bars them from psychiatric care. Conversely, the courts tend to go on perceiving their female offenders as 'relatively normal women', and it is often their apparent conformity and competence that make them so acceptable as psychiatric patients.

In place of such explanations, this study attributes the discrepancy to a complex and basically unintended interaction between two aspects of the legal and medical decision-making. On one hand there is the mass of social expectations about gender, that can radically modify the interpretation of criminal cases by both legal and medical personnel. On the other, and quite independently, there is the mass of legislative and institutional provisions, which do not in principle seek to favour one sex rather than the other, but which simply establish the various conditions that must be met, regardless of the subject's gender, before a psychiatric disposal can be made. The reason for the discrepancy cannot be found in either of these structures on its own: in fact there are aspects of each which would seem to move in the opposite direction, and favour the psychiatrization of *men*. To understand the discrepancy it is necessary to consider their *interaction*, and to unravel the (sometimes curious) arguments that bind them together in the course of medical and legal decision making.

The study is divided into two sections, of which the first looks at the impact of gender on the verdict, and the second at its impact on the sentence. In each half, the arguments are drawn initially from a detailed discussion of the structure of medico-legal provisions, and then 'fleshed out' through a close analysis of particular criminal cases. The conclusions suggest that the importance of the current imbalance lies not so much in the excess of psychiatry in relation to female offenders as its deficiency in relation to males. It is certainly true that many women now receive psychiatric disposals on the most slender of grounds, sometimes without even any diagnosed disorder. But more disturbing is that much larger numbers of undisputedly disordered male offenders are *refused* a psychiatric disposal, even in the face of obvious need for treatment, and sometimes in the face of a general consensus by all the professionals that a psychiatric disposal would be desirable. Although these unbalances become intelligible in the light of the particular contradictions and tensions of the existing context of medico-legal decisions, many of the decisions are individually bizarre and disturbing. The conclusion therefore argues for the need for radical changes in the whole organization of this aspect of criminal justice and psychiatry. And it suggests that equally valuable changes in the current unbalanced situation could be produced either through practical modifications in the structure of medico-legal provisions, or through challenging the medico-legal assumptions about the different natures and mentalities of male and female subjects.

Chapter one:

The discrepancy and its analysis

A young girl is robbed in a London street. Her assailants, a man and a woman, are jointly apprehended, jointly charged, and jointly brought to trial. Both are middle-aged, unemployed and black; both have extensive criminal records; both claim amnesia for the events in question, and are remanded for psychiatric and social reports.

On psychiatric examination, the woman is found to have a disturbed background, a history of drug and alcohol abuse, and various physical ailments, but is not regarded as ever having been psychiatrically ill. To quote from the psychiatric report:[1]

> There is no history of any psychiatric illness .... When I saw her she was very cooperative, answered questions as well as she could, and expressed regret at the events which led to her being charged .... There was no evidence of any gross abnormalities in her mental state, in particular she did not appear to be experiencing hallucinations or suffering from delusions, and in spite of her assertion that her memory is impaired, I could find no evidence of definite intellectual deterioration .... There is in my view no evidence of formal psychiatric illness.
>
> (Psychiatric report, case 41, woman charged with robbery)

The man, by contrast, is found to have a considerable psychiatric history, and to be suffering from a major mental illness at the time of the report:

> His psychiatric history dates back to 1968, [fifteen years prior to report] when he was treated at Hospital 1 with ECT.[2] At that time he was depressed and had persecutory ideas. Two years later he was seen at Hospital 2; by this time he had developed auditory hallucinations with many neurotic symptoms ... He was considered to show evidence of a personality disorder and to be an hysterical psychopath. In 1976 he was referred to Hospital 3 with symptoms of depression with paranoid ideas again; he was similarly referred to Hospital 3 in 1978; at that time he was considered to show unequivocal evidence of a schizophrenic illness. He was treated as an in-patient for two months and given injections to control his illness ... He was treated at Hospital 4 as an in-patient

between August 1982 and February 1983 ... he was considered to be suffering from mental illness, expressed bizarre delusional ideas that he was Prince Charles and that Princess Margaret was his mother, he claimed to hear the voice of Jesus. He responded to the appropriate treatment ... [and following his discharge] I was asked to take over his outpatient care ....

When I saw him [five months prior to the offence] he told me that he was very depressed [and] claimed to hear voices in his mind. His emotional responses were blunted and the picture is consistent with a diagnosis of chronic paranoid schizophrenia ....

This defendant has shown evidence of mental disorder for at least fifteen years with unequivocal evidence of schizophrenic illness .... It is quite impossible here to categorically state whether or not he is/was responsible for his actions. In my mind there is a reasonable doubt.

(Psychiatric report, case 123, male charged with robbery)

Each of the two defendants attempts to blame the offence on the other, but the jury decides that both defendants were participants in the crime, and both are convicted of it. The man is sentenced to two years' imprisonment. The woman is placed on probation, with a condition that she receive psychiatric treatment.

Viewed in relation to the particular medical findings of this case, the discrepancy in the sentencing may seem remarkable, even bizarre: a mentally ill offender is imprisoned for his crime, whilst his mentally fit accomplice is released to psychiatric care. Viewed against the overall pattern of criminal sentencing, however, the case is no more than an individual example of a much more general trend, whereby female defendants are consistently more likely than males to be referred for psychiatric examination, to be assessed as suitable subjects for psychiatric treatment, and ultimately to be dealt with by psychiatric means.

This book investigates this discrepancy, and traces the processes of medical and legal reasoning that produce and legitimate it. It is a book about the making of official decisions, the meaning of those decisions, the institutional constraints and personal assumptions that underlie them, and ultimately their justice.

A statistical overview

Under the terms of the criminal law, there exists a range of formal provisions whereby evidence of psychiatric abnormality may determine whether a defendant is found guilty of a particular offence, or justify the placing of a convicted offender under psychiatric care. These are the 'psychiatric disposals': the cases in which the outcome of the case is critically determined by psychiatric considerations. Figure 1 shows the proportion of male and female cases that have been dealt with through these provisions since 1950, and as can immediately be seen, the sexual discrepancy is both marked and

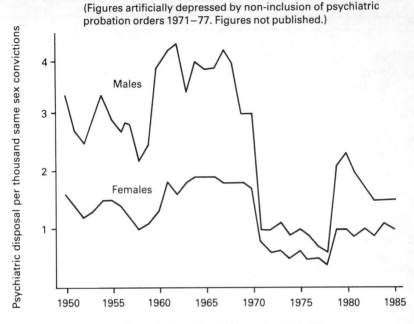

Figure 1: *Psychiatric Disposals, 1950–85*

stable. Despite noticeable fluctuations in the overall use of these provisions, the female rate remains consistently about twice that of the male.

At this point two very general observations may be made. First, in relation to the general field of sentencing decisions, these psychiatric disposals constitute such a tiny minority as to be numerically almost invisible. The highest rate shown is only 4.5 cases per thousand, and the lowest less than one case per thousand. At no point during this period have there been more than two and half thousand psychiatric disposals recorded in a year, as compared to annual conviction rates that now regularly exceed one and a half million. A potential problem in examining such a tiny section of the overall field is that from such a small initial base, even rather minor changes in the absolute number of psychiatric disposals could produce misleadingly large proportional swings. It is for this reason that I have taken my figures from a period spanning several decades. Within a single year, the level of variation that I am identifying could quite easily arise by chance, and be balanced by variations in the opposite direction in other years, but when viewed over several decades, the regularity and uniformity of the discrepancy is clearly too consistent over time to be dismissed in such a way.

Second, the discrepancy in the treatment of males and females only emerges when one considers the *rates* at which psychiatric provisions are used in either case. As illustrated in Figure 2, ordinary female convictions have been massively outnumbered by male throughout this period, and

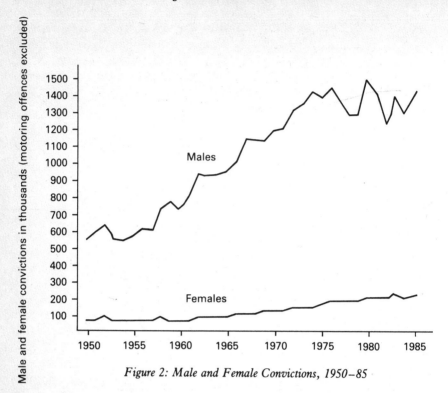

Figure 2: Male and Female Convictions, 1950–85

accordingly, in terms of absolute numbers, there are also more male than female psychiatric disposals per annum. In order to make accurate comparisons between the patterns of male and female disposal, it is therefore necessary to look at the difference in the *proportion* of male and female cases that are dealt with by psychiatric means, irrespective of overall differences in the numbers of males and females appearing before the courts.

Thus far I have been drawing a broad and deliberate distinction between the 'psychiatric' and the 'non-psychiatric' approach, and in so doing I have tended to homogenize the category of 'psychiatric disposals'. In one sense, this homogenization is both intentional and fundamental, in that I use this category to encompass all the forms of judicial outcome which depend upon the establishment of either a mental abnormality or a need for psychiatric treatment. This having been said, however, it should also be emphasized that the category of psychiatric disposals is a broad one, covering a heterogeneous field of juridical outcomes.

There are three main points at which psychiatric factors can play a part in deciding the outcome of a criminal case. First, the identification of the defendant as mentally disturbed can result in the pre-emptive discontinuation of legal proceedings prior to any conviction or acquittal. The police may take a suspected offender directly to a hospital, without initiating criminal charges,[3] or they may simply (as with any other offender) exercise the discretionary right not to prosecute.[4] Similarly, the Director of Public Prosecutions may drop charges on the basis of medical advice, or order an indefinite adjournment of the case.[5] Much more formally, once criminal proceedings have been instigated, a jury may find the defendant 'unfit to plead',[6] in which case he or she must be compulsorily admitted to hospital and detained until such time as the Secretary of State may authorize a release.

Second, psychiatric factors may be critical at the point of verdict, in determining whether the defendant is criminally responsible for illegal actions. Where a jury finds a defendant insane, (a condition defined by certain strict legal criteria and by no means equivalent to any modern psychiatric category), the defendant is by definition presumed to be incapable of criminal intent, and must be found 'not guilty by reason of insanity'. As with defendants found unfit to plead, this results in indefinite detention in a psychiatric hospital.[7] These provisions are used extremely rarely, and generally less than five such acquittals are recorded per year. Rather more common are cases where the individual is found to be suffering from 'diminished responsibility', a partial defence which is only available in cases of homicide, and which allows a conviction of murder to be reduced to one of manslaughter, still on grounds of mental abnormality, but an abnormality rather less extreme than is required for legal insanity. There are very similar legal provisions for cases of 'infanticide', where a mother kills her young infant whilst the 'balance of her mind' is judged to be disturbed as a result of pregnancy or lactation. Rather than the mandatory life sentence that must follow a murder conviction, offenders in either of these categories may be ordered to receive psychiatric treatment, or may be awarded any of the wide range of penal or rehabilitative sentences available in respect of manslaughter. I include these cases amongst psychiatric disposals whether or not compulsory treatment is ordered, since the very *form* of the conviction is based upon psychiatric definitions of the case.[8] The medical and legal considerations that arise in relation to these three verdicts are discussed in Chapters 2 and 3.

Finally, (and most importantly in terms of the numbers involved), there are those forms of psychiatric disposal which can be made only after a finding of guilt.[9] In these cases the convicted offender is ordered to receive psychiatric treatment either as a condition of a probation order or through a hospital order. In the latter case only, treatment must be as a formal (i.e. compulsorily detained) in-patient, and special restrictions may be imposed whereby the hospital may only release the offender with the permission of the Secretary of State. Where a psychiatric probation order is made, the patient may be treated as either an in-patient or an out-patient, and all treatment is technically on a voluntary basis. However, once the offender has agreed to the order being made, a refusal to accept any 'reasonable'[10] treatment places the defendant in breach of probation, and thus makes him or her liable to the reinstatement of penal sanctions.

Although it is only in these limited criminal cases that psychiatric considerations are privileged, psychiatry's involvement in criminal justice extends far beyond this field. Historically, the relationship between psychiatry and criminal justice is a long and complex one, of which the explicit 'psychiatrization' of a small number of individual cases is only the most public aspect. Additionally, psychiatry provides the criminal justice system with both a general expertise in the psychology of crime and punishment, (hence, for example, the frequent requests for psychiatric assessment even in cases where no psychiatric disposal is under consideration), and also a specialized service for the medical management of the more disturbed and recalcitrant of the prison population. Historically it was this kind of involvement of psychiatry *within* the criminal justice system that provided the conditions for both the modification of the old provisions for the criminally deranged, and the development of the various new forms of psychiatric disposal. More recently, the continuing involvement of psychiatry in penal establishments (offering at least a nominal assurance that prisoners will be accorded psychiatric attention if necessary) is amongst the factors that influence many modern decisions *not* to make a formal psychiatric disposal. In analysing the final distribution of disposals, it will therefore also be necessary to consider these more general relationships between penality and psychiatry, and to take into account this shadowy obverse of psychiatric sentencing whereby many mentally disturbed offenders are committed to the uncertain facilities of the prison medical service. The whole territory of these post-conviction disposals is discussed in Chapters 4, 5 and 6.

This chapter began with the simple observation of a general sexual imbalance in the use of psychiatric disposals. An analysis of the various *forms* of psychiatric disposal, however, reveals a still further differentiation. Figure 3 shows the various disposals which entail a specific requirement of

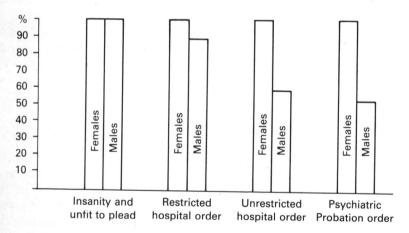

Figure 3: Male Rate of Psychiatric Disposal as a Percentage of Female Rate, by type of disposal, 1980–84

psychiatric treatment (excluding diminished responsibility or infanticide cases, which may or may not be dealt with by an order for psychiatric treatment). The diagram is arranged according to the degree of psychiatric surveillance and coercion that each disposal entails. The male rate is shown as a percentage of the female rate for each type of disposal, after adjustment for the difference in the absolute numbers of male and female cases involved.

From this it can clearly be seen that the excess of psychiatry in the disposal of female cases is not uniformly distributed across all the forms of psychiatric disposal, but is in fact concentrated at the lowest level of psychiatric involvement, in the least restrictive and most consensual forms of treatment. Starting at the most coercive extreme, the insanity verdict and the finding of unfitness to plead, (both of which entail mandatory and indefinite psychiatric detention), there is no significant difference between the male and the female rate. As one proceeds along this continuum, however, the discrepancy becomes progressively more marked, with the greatest excess of females being found in the least coercive form of disposal, that of the psychiatric probation order.

An analogous pattern emerges in the sentencing of the diminished responsibility and infanticide cases. About half the female convicts are awarded a probation order, often with some form of psychiatric arrangement, whilst only a handful are ever imprisoned or detained in hospital under a restriction order. The equivalent male cases, conversely, are very rarely given probation orders. The commonest disposal in male cases is imprisonment, and the majority of those who do receive orders for psychiatric treatment are subjected to a restriction order, and treated under conditions of secure detention.[11]

Explaining and obscuring

These sexual discrepancies in the use of psychiatric disposals have been largely ignored in the literature in this field. Where the discrepancy is noted at all, it has almost invariably been in terms which simply incorporate it into other more general arguments about the relationships between gender and crime or gender and psychiatry. Such an approach is, I suggest, quite misleading.

Mental morbidity and sexual differences

Perhaps the most obvious way of 'explaining' the comparatively high rate of psychiatric disposals amongst female offenders is by reference to the comparatively high rate of psychiatric morbidity amongst women *in general*. There is consistent evidence[12] that women report more psychiatric symptoms than do men, are more frequently diagnosed as mentally disordered, and are more frequently subjected to psychiatric treatment of every kind. On this basis, the comparatively high rate of psychiatric disposal of female offenders has in various texts[13] been noted as if merely the predictable outcome of prior differences in the mental morbidity of the male and female populations, transposed onto the particular population of the criminal courts.

The first objection to such an explanation is that the apparent excess of psychiatric involvement with female offenders is actually much greater than the excess in female morbidity generally. Even in the most divergent estimates of male and female morbidity, the apparent excess of females never reaches the two-to-one ratio that one finds in psychiatric disposals through the courts. One would have to assume, therefore, that even compared to the general population of women, (who are in any case assumed to be more mentally unstable than men), female offenders carry an *excessive* burden of mental instability. In terms of its immediate correspondence with the conventional wisdom of criminology[14] (in which the criminal woman is almost by definition mentally abnormal) this line of explanation is obviously attractive. Psychological studies of criminal women have almost invariably reported unusually high levels of psychopathology,[15] and it is easy to glide from this observation to the assumption that this is what must account for their high rate of psychiatric disposal. Simple and convincing though this line of explanation may seem, it is deeply flawed.

First there is the way in which this argument treats psychiatric disorder as an objective characteristic of the subject, that is simply 'there', awaiting medical diagnosis and independent of either the observer or the framework of observation. This conception of mental disorder has been repeatedly exposed as untenable,[16] and an argument which bases itself upon it is therefore theoretically suspect from the start. The categories of mental disorders, illnesses and abnormalities are socially constructed; it is psychiatry that both produces this grid of mental morbidity, and distributes its male and female subjects within it. In seeking to explain psychiatry's differential involvement with its male and female subjects, it is therefore theoretically illogical to appeal to the 'prior' mental health of these subjects, or their 'prior' positioning within that grid. If we are to understand these differences, we must ask instead what it is about the practice of psychiatry that allows and produces this differentiation.

In order to do so, one must consider how the psychiatrization of offenders actually takes place, at the empirical level of the practical and procedural organization of psychiatry and criminal justice. The line of argument that makes the mental pathology of offenders the simple determinant of psychiatric disposals not only assumes that states of mental pathology have an objective existence, but also, equally problematically, that there is both a direct correspondence between the presence of these 'objective disorders' and their detection, and a further correspondence between this detection and the decision to impose a psychiatric disposal. Both assumptions are necessary in order to sustain the original argument, but if one considers the concrete settings in which offenders are selected for such treatment, both must be rejected.

First, there is no justification for assuming that any mental disorder of the defendant will necessarily come to the notice of the relevant authorities. With the exception of subjects accused of murder, there is no routine psychiatric 'screening' of defendants, and less than 5 per cent of all defendants will be exposed to any professional psychiatric scrutiny.[17] It is of course impossible to estimate how many of the remaining 95 per cent might be diagnosed as disordered if they *were* to be psychiatrically assessed. The selection of the privileged 5 per cent is almost exclusively dependent upon lay assessments of the case by criminal justice personnel, who have no psychiatric training, and whose contact with the defendant is normally both brief and preoccupied by quite different concerns. Under such conditions there is no reason to assume either that all the relevant cases will be correctly identified, or that the personnel concerned will be equally accurate (or inaccurate) in their assessment of male and female cases. As I discuss in Chapter 6 there are certainly sexual differences in the proportion of these lay assessments that are subsequently confirmed by medical diagnosis.

Second, there is the problem of assuming a direct and sexually undifferentiated correspondence between the detection of disorder and the imposition of a psychiatric disposal. This assumption is simply wrong. As I shall discuss in Chapters 5 and 6, the large majority of cases where the offender is medically assessed and diagnosed as disordered do *not* result in any psychiatric disposal. Furthermore, it is quite possible for a psychiatric disposal to be made in the *absence* of any diagnosis of disorder. And finally, the relationship between the application of a medical diagnosis and the imposition of a psychiatric disposal is not the same for male and female cases: a smaller proportion of diagnosed male cases are subjected to psychiatric orders than of diagnosed female cases, whilst the use of psychiatric disposals for non-diagnosed cases is largely restricted to female cases.

Thus at every turn the attempt to explain the sexual discrepancy in sentencing by reference to prior differences in the psychopathology of male and female offenders is invalidated by an attention to the *social* conditions under which psychiatric disposals are made. And it is to these social conditions that we must turn in making sense of the distribution of these disposals.

Chivalry and chauvinism

At this stage, the ground of explanation shifts from the field of medical epidemiology to that of the sociology of deviance and social control, and from the different mentalities of male and female criminals to the different approaches of medicine and criminal justice towards their male and female subjects. A number of sociological arguments already converge on this field, and although this study ultimately rejects many of their assumptions, they provide an important point of departure for the analysis that this study proposes.

On the legal and criminological side, there are various discussions which address the apparent reluctance of criminal justice agents either to criminalize women or to expose them to the full force of criminal sanctions. The arguments proposed in these discussions, although diverse in their political allegiances, are remarkably consistent in their structure. In each case, they rest on the proposition of a general relationship between gender and criminal justice, in which the different treatment of male and female subjects, (throughout the law's field of operation and not specifically in relation to psychiatric involvement), can be attributed to the influence of male attitudes and interests. The more conservative texts emphasize the 'chivalry' of male attitudes, and attribute the differential treatment of female offenders to a more or less benevolent[18] protectiveness towards women, which is assumed to operate, albeit unfairly, to their general advantage. When addressed within these general arguments, (if, indeed, addressed at all),[19] the apparently disproportionate use of psychiatric measures for female offenders is routinely elided with a general tendency towards rehabilitative measures, which in turn is conceived as a form of judicial leniency. Psychiatric explanations offer at least a partial exculpation, which can exempt the offender from the full force of legal sanctions and provide a less punitive outcome. This anodyne perspective is flatly rejected by more radical and feminist authors, who predictably offer a more sinister interpretation of the differential treatment of female offenders. They argue that any apparent 'favouritism' of the law towards its female subjects[20] is in fact motivated by patriarchal interests. On one hand, they interpret any objective lenience towards female offenders as merely a device whereby patriarchal agents attempt to obscure the potential power of women. The failure to punish women is seen as a means of denying or trivializing any threat women's action might pose to social order, and thus invalidating the political meanings of women's deviance. On the other hand, the preference for 'rehabilitative' approaches for female offenders is interpreted as a means both of reasserting the dependency of female offenders, and of covertly punishing and controlling them. In this context, it is the potentially coercive aspects of psychiatric treatment that are stressed: in certain cases a psychiatric disposal may entail longer incarceration, or more intrusive surveillance, or greater stigmatization than would be entailed by an alternative penal measure.

At this point, the argument intersects with a body of feminist argument, initially developed by Phyllis Chesler, which theorizes all psychiatric activity in terms of its contribution to patriarchal oppression. What Chesler proposes is that there is an inherent relationship between gender and psychiatry, such that the fundamental function of psychiatry is the policing of femininity and the oppressive preservation of conventional gender stereotypes. Following the earlier arguments of Broverman *et al.*,[21] Chesler begins from the premiss that what constitutes the conventional 'feminine role' are characteristics and behaviours which are ultimately incompatible with ideals of mental health – self-destructiveness, self-denial, passivity, timidity, over-emotionalism, triviality, childishness and so on. On this basis, she goes on to argue that what psychiatry pathologizes are on one hand the unhealthy traits which the majority of women are routinely coerced into adopting, and on the other the various behaviours by which a minority of women attempt to refuse or reject such traits. Chesler puts it thus:

> What we consider 'madness' whether it appears in women or in men, is either the acting out of the devalued female role or the total or partial rejection of one's sex role stereotype. Women who act out the conditioned female role are clinically viewed as 'neurotic' or 'psychotic'. Hospitalization is for predominantly female behaviours: depression, suicide attempts, anxiety neuroses, paranoia or promiscuity. Women who reject or are ambivalent about the female role frighten both themselves and society, and are probably ostracized at an early age. Hospitalization is for less female behaviours: schizophrenia, lesbianism, or promiscuity. Men who act out the female role and who for example are 'dependent', 'passive', sexually and physically 'fearful' or 'inactive' are also seen as 'neurotic' or 'psychotic'. If hospitalized they are usually labelled as 'schizophrenic' or 'homosexual'. Men who act out the male role – but who are too young, too poor or too black are usually incarcerated as 'criminals' or 'sociopaths' rather than as schizophrenics or neurotics.
>
> (Chesler, 1974, p. 56–7)

Despite the apparent aptness of this analysis to my investigations, offering as it appears to do an obvious basis from which to look at the inequalities of psychiatric treatment for male and female offenders, I consider it neither correct nor useful. In the first place, as I have argued at length elsewhere,[22] Chesler's analysis of the psychiatric project bears little relation to the actual practice of modern psychiatry. Modern psychiatry is certainly riddled with sexist assumptions and guilty of numerous failings in its dealings with women patients, but it nowhere conforms to that single-minded preoccupation with gender role, that Chesler proposes as its fundamental and essential feature. In the second place, any attempt to apply Chesler's analysis to a forensic context produces specific and more immediate problems.

Firstly, there is an obvious problem of 'overkill'. According to this model, the basis of the psychiatrization of female offenders is either their 'acting out' of the prescribed female role or their rejection of some or all aspects of it. Put these two categories together and they cover the entire field, embracing all female offenders, if not the entire population of women. We have therefore a formula which will explain the treatment of all those female offenders who are dealt with by psychiatric measures (actually less than 1 per cent of the total), but only at the expense of generating a much larger problem of how the other 99 per cent manage to escape. And when one attempts to apply this model to the treatment of men, precisely the opposite problem arises: it becomes difficult to understand how any male offenders come to be treated by psychiatric means at all. The only circumstances in which Chesler anticipates the psychiatrization of males are those under which they (perversely, and against their own interests) adopt the devalued female role. This line of argument may be just about applicable to the occasional psychiatrization of male shoplifters or exhibitionists, but is impossible to reconcile with the fact that the majority of male psychiatric disposals are for cases involving personal violence, destruction of property and sexual aggression.

There is, however, an even more immediate problem in the attempt to explain sexual differences in the treatment of offenders by reference to some general force of sexual oppression, as is implied both by Chesler's analysis and by the earlier arguments about judicial paternalism. Such an explanation demands as its intitial premiss the assertion of 'the patriarchy', as an all-embracing, all-powerful system of male dictatorship, which determines, more or less violently, all the forms and outcomes of social relations, including those of psychiatry and the law. This is certainly a convenient way to explain away all the discrepancies in the treatment of men and women. But as several authors have argued, (notably Adams and Cousins),[23] it is fundamentally flawed. To explain the existence of each individual sexual division simply by asserting the pre-existence of another all-encompassing one is to create an argument that is theoretically circular and politically numb.

At a substantive level, it blurs the edges of all the specific questions that might otherwise be asked about the nature and extent and form of this discrepancy in sentencing, by unifying it with all the other social divisions of gender, wherever and however they occur. The assumption that all social relations are predetermined by a general oppression of all women by all men converts any specific discussion of this or any other sexual discrepancy into an otiose restatement of what is already presumed in advance. In the process, it dismisses as insignificant all the more specific and problematic questions that one might otherwise wish to ask, such as why only some of these (uniformly oppressed and homogeneously constructed) female subjects are exposed to this differential psychiatrization, or why the various (monolithically patriarchal) agencies involved in these discriminations should ever come into disagreement. This is a form of analysis which lends a surface of intelligibility to everything in general – behind which everything in particular seems suddenly indistinct.

Politically this kind of analysis has the same anaesthetizing effect. In the first place, it pre-empts any question as to the political valency of the discrepancy: psychiatry and the law are both conceived as merely instances of the patriarchy, so whatever either of them does must by definition be oppressive towards women and advantageous to men. It will thus be redundant to this analysis to ask whether the psychiatrization of female offenders might in certain circumstances operate to their advantage, or whether the reluctance to provide psychiatric care for male offenders might indicate a political failing. The oppressive nature of the psychiatrization of female offenders is necessarily assumed in advance of any analysis – just as the benificence of psychiatry would necessarily have been presumed had it been males who were more typically afforded such treatment. Moreover, this form of analysis also robs political questioning of any practical significance. If all structures of authority, such as medicine and the law, are assumed to be fundamentally predetermined by the forces of patriarchy, then there is no point in attempting to weigh up the various advantages and disadvantages of different social practices, let alone to intervene in them. Short of a total revolution, all political action becomes pointless; from this perspective any attempt to reconstruct the practices of psychiatry or the law must be dismissed as merely cosmetic or reformist.

Such an approach is simply not useful, and the only way to avoid its cul-de-sac of analysis is to refuse its assumptions from the outset. The world is full of sexism, but this sexism does not operate uniformly nor inexorably nor by any super-human machinery. Other principles sometimes subvert it (principles of order and control, for example, which coerce men no less than women), and at times it subverts itself, (as when sexist assumptions of women's frailty, which elsewhere operate to women's detriment, are tactically employed to their advantage).[24] My analysis will not dispute that decisions about the disposal of male and female cases are powerfully influenced by sexist assumptions. On the contrary, one of my main aims is to expose and describe such assumptions in operation. But there is no reason to assume that the outcome of these processes will be entirely predictable and unambiguous. A careful assessment of the disparites would probably find long-term disadvantages for women in their easy psychiatrization – but a more immediate cause for disquiet might be the refusal of psychiatric treatment to many of the men.

An alternative analysis

The phenomenon addressed in this book is both specific and localized. It comprises a pattern of social decisions that can be precisely identified and delimited, and that arises within concrete and specifiable institutional contexts. My analysis is similarly specific and localized: the sexual discrepancy is examined through an investigation of the decision-making processes that concretely generate it.

Conceptually and methodologically, this investigation owes much to the approach developed by Michel Foucault.[25] It is an investigation at the level of the *discourses* of medicine and the law. In referring to 'discourses' I am acknowledging the centrality of language in the social processes that lead to these disposals, but I am also asserting that there is more at stake in this field than 'mere words'. The 'discourse' of medicine and law are much more than collections of documents or disembodied exchanges of legal and medical 'talk'. They are structures of knowledge through which members of these professions understand and decide things. They are structures of social relationship which establish different obligations and authorities for different categories of person, such as patients, offenders, doctors, judges, probation officers and so on. They are impersonal forms, existing independently of any of these persons 'as individuals'. They are historical and political frameworks of social organization, that make some social actions possible whilst precluding others. In a simple and accessible sense, the discourses of medicine and the law are what lawyers and doctors were referring to when they explained their decisions and actions by telling me: 'It's the system'.

In speaking of discourse, I am therefore referring to the whole *systematicity* of medicine and the law. The recordable, analysable statements that are produced within medicine and the law give concrete access to this systematicity, and these medical and legal statements therefore provide the substantive material of my study. In the course of this book I assemble various bodies of medical and legal texts, from legal statutes, court transcripts, medical reports, and so on, and some of these I cut up and examine in quite minute and surgical detail. But this 'analysis of discourse' is not intended as simply 'literary criticism'. It is an analysis that belongs to the concrete world of serious everyday decisions. It is an attempt to make sense of how this pattern of decisions can arise; to identify the constraints that preclude other (perhaps 'better') decisions from being made; and to question what would have to be changed before this 'system' could operate differently. The motivations of this examination are therefore political as well as intellectual.

This is enough about the theoretical and methodological underpinnings of this study.[26] It will suffice at this point to underline certain premises which are fundamental to this approach, and which inform my analysis at every stage. First, as I have indicated, this approach asserts that these patterns of medico-legal decisions do not appear out of thin air, but are produced through quite concrete, everyday activities of medical and judicial personnel. In this sense the phenomenon to be examined is 'objective' and 'observable', and the analysis can proceed along a straightforward and positivist path.[27] What appears rather abstractly as an 'official statistic' or a 'social trend' in the medicalization of female offenders can be analysed in terms of a quite material production of social decisions. This is not to suggest, however, that the sexual discrepancy in these decisions can be understood as simply an expression of the personal perceptions, preferences and prejudices of the agents concerned. For the second premiss of this analysis is that neither doctors nor sentencers are free to make just *any* decision, according to their personal whim: they are constrained at every turn by the impersonal regularities of the medical and judicial discourses within which they work and speak. The analysis identifies and describes these 'impersonal regularities' and the decisions to which they lead.

This entails an investigation at a number of different levels and in a number of different directions. It requires an analysis of the formal provisions of psychiatric disposals, and of the practical arrangements for psychiatric contact with offenders. It involves taking account of the wider historical and social context of these provisions. And it focuses on the forms of assessment, evidence, categorization and reasoning that determine which particular offenders are selected for this special psychiatric treatment.

Substantively this analysis draws on three main bodies of material. In relation to each, fuller details are given both in the main body of the chapters where the material is discussed and in the Appendices. First, there are the formal provisions of the law, the jurisprudential doctrines that organize their interpretation and the official instruments and guidelines that regulate their application. Throughout the study, these provide a key reference point for my discussion, and in the second and fourth chapters, they comprise the main material of analysis.

The heart of the analysis comprises a detailed examination of documents concerning specific male and female cases. Much of this material is drawn from official court files – including case summaries, record sheets, psychiatric and social reports, records of police interrogations, special legal advice and instructions. Additionally, I refer to a number of reported cases, to transcripts of certain court proceedings, and to my own observations of particular cases. The selection of cases was motivated by a variety of theoretical and practical concerns, which are discussed in Appendix B. At a simple and immediate level it must be noted from the outset that the sample was intended to provide a sound basis for a specific and qualitative analysis, rather than a large-scale or statistical one. It is therefore small and selected by non-random criteria; it cannot be taken as statistically representative. Appendix B gives information on each of the 129 cases examined in detail, which may be summarized as follows:

1. 25 male and 24 female homicide cases, drawn randomly.
2. 11 male homicides involving 'domestic' killings.
3. 33 male and 36 female cases all of which were referred for psychiatric assessment, and from which psychiatric reports were available. These were selected from amongst the following offence groups: acquisitive offences such as theft and burglary; assaults and woundings; criminal damage and arson.

Finally, there is material drawn from discussions and interviews with the various groups of professional personnel. In the course of my investigation I was able to share many informal conversations with professional workers, including lawyers, probation officers, magistrates, judges, senior police officials and police officers on court duty, clerks of court, psychiatrists, hospital managers and prison personnel. Additionally, I conducted a series of thirty-four semi-structured interviews with lawyers, probation officers, magistrates, and psychiatrists. The object of these interviews was to illuminate how members of these professional groups conceived of such issues as mental abnormality, its relation to crime, the appropriate circumstances for invoking psychiatric involvement that might typically arise. These interviews, like my observations and records of informal discussions with professional staff, were not used for detailed analysis but provided a wealth of background information and illustrations. My general framework of questions is set out in Appendix C.

In relation to each of these bodies of material, I pose two complementary questions. First, I ask how it is that any particular case either does or does not come to be organized in psychiatric terms: what discursive processes allow psychiatric considerations to be privileged in one case rather than another? Second, I ask whether these discursive processes operate in the same way in male and female cases, and if not, in what way they are different and what impact this has on the overall process of decision. These two questions take on different aspects in relation to the different levels and directions of the analysis, but their basic preoccupations remain the same throughout, and their recurring formulations and reformulations provide the lines of continuity which link the various discussions and arguments of this text.

Notes

1 In all material quoted from individual case records, references to named individuals or institutions have been either omitted or altered. All names appearing in these extracts are fictional.

2 Electro-convulsive therapy; a medical treatment routinely (though controversially) used for severe depressive conditions.

3 Mental Health Act 1983, s 136. The use of these powers is not dealt with in this study, which is confined to cases which actually come to court. See Walker and McCabe (1973, p. 251f) for an informative discussion of this area.

4 This approach has become increasingly popular, and some police forces have adopted carefully planned strategies to avoid the prosecution of the mentally disordered and other 'at risk' offenders. See Harris (1981).

5 Home Office Circular 26/1983 indicates the circumstances in which the Director of Public Prosecutions might choose not to proceed with a prosecution. These include cases where the alleged offender 'is suffering from some form of mental illness and the strain of criminal proceedings will lead to a considerable worsening of his condition'.

6 Criminal Lunatics Act 1800, s 2; Criminal Procedure (Insanity) Act 1964.

7 This indefinite detention 'at Her Majesty's pleasure' *may* mean permanent medical incarceration, but it need not necessarily do so. The Secretary of State authorizes a handful of releases most years.

8 See Appendix A, note 3.

9 A hospital order can occasionally be made *without* a conviction being formally recorded, provided that the *grounds* for a conviction have been established; (Mental Health Act 1983, s 37 (3)); see Walker and McCabe (1973, p. 104).

10 The Criminal Justice Act 1948, s 6(6) establishes that a probationer shall not be held in breach of such an order if he has refused only such treatment, including surgical or electrical treatment, as the court regards it as reasonable to refuse.

11 These comments are based on cumulated figures drawn from the Criminal Satistics for England and Wales 1979–85, since the annual numbers are small. See also outcomes of homicide cases in my own sample, Table 2, Appendix B.

12 See DHSS Mental Health Statistics (annual publication). A useful and critical review on epidemiological findings on women's mental health is provided by Busfield (1983).

13 See Walker and McCabe (1973, p. 256); D'Orban (1971).

14 This notion gained increasing currency from the 1950s to 1970s and informs much of the work on female crime during this period, e.g. Konopka (1966), Cowie *et al.* (1968).

15 These findings are helpfully reviewed in D'Orban (1971).

16 e.g. Hirst and Woolley (1982, Part 2) which provides a particularly clear discussion of these arguments. See also Foucault 1972 p. 40f.

17 Dell and Gibbens (1971); Gibbens *et al.* (1977); Walker and McCabe (1973). No official statistics are published regarding the number of cases where psychiatric reports are prepared on bail, but the Prison Service publishes annual figures on the number of reports prepared in custody; see Home Office, Prison Statistics.

18 Pollak (1950) is the original proponent of this theory, which has been reproduced in conservative quarters ever since.

19 See Smart (1976). Anderson (1976) provides a general review of the feminist literature on the 'chivalry' debate.

20 Anderson, ibid. See also Chesney-Lind (1977, 1978) who argues that in fact women are *not* treated more leniently.

21 Chesler (1974); Broverman *et al.* (1970). See also A1–Issa (1980) for discussion of this material.

22 Allen (1986).

23 e.g. Adams and Minson (1978); Cousins (1980).

24 See Cousins (1980) for a general discussion of the non-monolithic nature of the law, and its lack of any homogeneous approach to issues of gender.

25 Foucault (1972) passim.

26 The reader who is already familiar with this approach will probably recognize how its preoccupations have structured this study. Throughout this book I have endeavoured, however, to present the analysis in terms which are accessible to the general reader, and which require no familiarity with the complexities of discourse theory.

27 See Foucault (1972) p. 125, for a discussion of the limits of this 'positivism' of discourse analysis.

Chapter two:

Responsibility and the verdict

> Every man is presumed to be sane and to possess a sufficient degree of reason to
> be responsible for his crimes until the contrary be proved to the jury's
> satisfaction ... to establish a defence of insanity, it must clearly be proved that
> the party accused was labouring under such a defect of reason, from disease of
> the mind, as not to know the nature of the act, or if he did know it, that he did
> not know that he was doing what was wrong.
>
> (M'Naghten Rules, 10 Cl & F,[1] at 120)

Historically it was in relation to the *verdict* of the trial that considerations of
the subject's mentality first came to have a special significance for the
criminal law. In order for a subject to be legally convicted of a crime, he or
she must be constituted as *criminally responsible* for the act in question, and
this state of responsibility is formally dependent upon the subject's
possession of certain specific mental faculties, operating in certain specific
ways.

These are faculties in which the madman or the imbecile may be declared
defective. It is this possibility that underlies a series of provisions whereby
evidence of mental abnormality provides ground for a special *verdict* to be
passed – as in the findings of insanity, diminished responsibility and
infacticide.

Whether the subject is normal or abnormal, legally guilty or innocent, the
verdict thus depends upon a specific assessment of his or her mental state.
This chapter is about the terms in which the law requires this assessment to
take place. It describes the legal notions of normal and abnormal mentality,
and looks at the part played by gender in the construction of these terms. Its
immediate object is to demonstrate the background of legal concepts and
questions which are at issue in the specific legal cases analysed in the next
chapter. More generally, it seeks to illuminate the 'model of the person' that
is taken for granted in judicial discussion, and that underpins the whole field
of decisions discussed in this text.

Mentality and the normal subjects of the law

The question of 'responsibility' introduces a psychological dimension into the construction of nearly every criminal case. Under English law, crimes are almost never defined in purely behavioural terms,[2] but require the coincidence of a particular prohibited behaviour and some specified state of mind. This coincidence is often expressed in terms of two 'components' of a crime, the 'wrongful deed' or *actus reus*, and the 'wrongful mind', the *mens rea*. Unless both of these components are satisfactorily established during the trial, then technically no crime has been proven, and the defendant must be acquitted as innocent. What then are the components of this 'culpable state of mind'? What psychological faculties are presumed to sustain this normal state of responsibility?

Intentionality, foresight, understanding

Throughout the formulation of the criminal law, there is a privileging of the faculty of *intention*. The legal subject is an intending subject, and it is through a notion of intentionality that legal discourse establishes its crucial relationship between an inner domain of mentality and an outer domain of behaviour. 'Intention' can be conceived as that movement of the will whereby the internal contents of minds (thoughts, motives, desires, and so on) come to be translated into external deeds. And the court will be required to make certain judgments about the nature of these 'mental contents', in order to determine what crime, if any, a wrongful deed amounts to. For example, if a woman has set light to a house in which others are sleeping, she may, depending on what was in her mind at the time, have committed no crime at all (if the act was merely accidental), or the crime of simple arson (if she intended only to cause damage to property), or the more serious crime of arson with recklessness as to whether life was endangered or with intent to endanger life, or even, in the extreme case, the crime of actual or attempted murder.

The smallest degree of intentionality which will suffice to bring the subject into the ambit of the criminal law is that of 'negligence'. Negligence, (on grounds of which a person can be found guilty of many offences, notably manslaughter), may be defined as a failure on the part of the subject to govern his or her behaviour 'with the care, skill or foresight that a reasonable man in his situation would exercise', or as 'non-compliance with a standard of conduct in relation to a risk which is reasonably intelligible'.[3] Minimally, the concept of criminal responsibility thus assumes a subject with the necessary intellectual capacity to foresee certain possible outcomes of behaviour, and to regulate his or her behaviour accordingly.

The graver notion of 'recklessness' introduces two more positive components: an *actual* foresight as to the potential consequences of action, and an actual understanding that certain of these outcomes may be legally prohibited.[4] For example, a defendant might be found to have recklessly caused the death of another, if he or she sets fire to a house, having foreseen that it might possibly be occupied and that lives might thus be endangered. It will be immaterial here whether the defendant hopes that the house is occupied or not, or has any wish to cause injury. All that is necessary is that the defendant is assessed as having been *aware* of the possibility.

The strongest degree of intentionality is that of 'specific intent', as is required, for example, in order to establish the crime of murder. A specific criminal intent requires a subject who correctly foresees and understands the likely consequences of behaviour, and yet purposively performs that behaviour, with the distinct and wilful objective of achieving those consequences, knowing them to be prohibited by the law. Although the lesser levels of intentionality are all that need be demonstrated for many offences, it is this full intentionality, in which knowledge and will and action coincide, that the law takes for granted as the normal state of legal subjects. The law irrebuttably presumes that legal subjects have knowledge of the law of the land: thus defendants cannot excuse themselves by claiming ignorance of the law. The law also assumes that legal subjects normally foresee and intend the 'natural and probable' outcomes of their behaviour. This presumption, however, is rebuttable by contrary evidence, and the test of it is always a 'subjective' one,[5] as provided for in the Criminal Justice Act 1967:

> A court or jury in determining whether a person has committed an offence,
>   (a) shall not be bound in law to infer that he intended or foresaw a result of his actions by reason only of it being a natural and probable consequence of those actions; but
>   (b) shall decide whether he did intend and foresee that result by reference to all the evidence drawing such inferences from the evidence as appear proper in the circumstances.
>
> (Criminal Justice Act, 1967, s 8)

The court is thus concerned with assessing what was actually in the defendant's mind. If evidence is brought that intention and foresight were not in fact present (however bizarre this absence might seem), the court is at liberty to accept this evidence, and to base its verdict upon it.

As these observations indicate, the legal conception of guilt is predicated on a complex of interrelationships between understanding, foresight, will and action, in which each link must in each case be present in order for guilt to be properly established. It therefore follows that various failures of this linkage should exclude or reduce guilt, as in the case of accidental behaviour (absence of connection between behaviour and will), or mistake (absence of connection between action and understanding).[6] Of the various permutations of such failures, those that primarily concern us are those where the break in the link is some mental condition of the subject, held to be qualitatively foreign to the legal norm of intentional subjectivity. Several such legally abnormal states (only some of which involve any notion of strictly *medical* pathology) are defined in the criminal law, and may provide a defence or partial defence against guilt.

Automatism, provocation, duress: the frailty of the normal

The state of automatism is one where behaviour has in some way become detached from the exercise of the will.

> What is missing in these cases appears to most people as a vital link between mind and body; and both the ordinary man and the lawyer might well insist on this by saying that in these cases there is not 'really' a human action at all, and certainly nothing for which anyone should be made criminally responsible.
>
> (H. L. A. Hart, Jubilee Lectures)[7]

The law holds that such behaviour can arise even in a normal subject, as in the involuntary movements of reflex actions, spasms, tics, or somnambulism,[8] and a person who performs some prohibited action in the course of such movements must be simply acquitted.

In automatism, there is a simple lack of intentionality: the behaviour of the body has no relation to any contents of the mind. In duress and provocation, by contrast, intentions are present, but these are related to mental contents that are both exceptional and alien to the subject's normal state of mind. Like automatism, the establishment of 'duress' offers a complete defence, and so must result in an acquittal.[9] A defendant may be deemed to have acted under duress, if, at the point of committing the wrongful deed, he or she is acting under an immediate and inescapable threat of violence that effectively 'neutralizes the will',[10] and might similarly neutralize the will of any normal, reasonable person. Under conditions of duress, the subject's behaviour is attributed to mental pressures more compelling than those of lawful self-control:

> The law must recognize that the instinct ... of self-preservation is powerful and natural, and that it would be censorious and inhumane if it did not recognize the appalling plight of a person who perhaps suddenly finds his life in jeopardy unless he submits and obeys.
>
> (Law Commission, 1977, para 2.16)

The defence of provocation is conceptually similar, but is restricted to cases of homicide and provides only a partial defence, allowing a reduction of the crime from murder to manslaughter. The Homicide Act 1957 lays down two criteria that must both be met for this defence. First it must be established that the defendant was subjected to such provocation as would cause a reasonable person to lose self-control, and second that the homicide was committed whilst the defendant *was* in fact out of control by virtue of the provocation. In the classic formulation by Judge Devlin, the condition of provocation is described as rendering the accused 'so subject to passion as to make him or her for the moment not master of his mind'.[11]

The reasonable man

The notion of the 'reasonable man' appears repeatedly in these legal provisions: in the context of recklessness, provocation and duress, and even, as I shall discuss in a moment, in relation to diminished responsibility. This concept of the 'reasonable man' is intended to provide an objective standard of comparison beside which the subjective state of legal subjects can be judged. It forms the basis of the so-called 'objective tests' that are required by several of the legal provisions relating to the assessment of criminal responsibility.

Where the law demands such a test, the court must consider not only the 'subjective' question of what the defendant was actually experiencing at the time in question, but also the so-called 'objective' question of whether, under similar circumstances, a 'reasonable man' might have had a similar psychological response. The main object of this dual test is the prevention of a situation in which, for example, a particularly excitable or bad-tempered person might be granted a defence which would be unavailable to one of more quiet and equable temperament.[12]

In principle, and as the test was originally applied, the notion of the 'reasonable man' establishes a single, consistent and uniform yardstick, against which the legal acceptability of individual responses might be measured, irrespective of the personal attributes of the defendant. In practice, however, the situation is more complicated, and has become steadily more so over the last ten years. The change can be traced not only in judgments concerning provocation to homicide, but also in other cases, such as those involving the defence of duress.[13]

The change may be traced through a number of moves. As a point of departure we might consider a Crown Court ruling[14] to the effect that in deciding whether the defence of provocation could be applied to a fifteen-year-old boy, what the jury had to consider was whether:

> ... the provocation was sufficient to make a reasonable man in like circumstances behave as the defendant did. Not a reasonable boy ... or a reasonable lad; it is an objective test – a reasonable man.
>
> (*Camplin*, 1978, 1 All ER 1236)

This is the objective test in its pure form, in which a single yardstick of comparison (apparently the assumed response of a normal adult male) is applied without regard to whether the defendant shares such characteristics. This judgment, however, was overturned by the Court of Appeal, which ruled that in order for the defence to stand:

> ... the proper direction to the jury is to invite the jury to consider whether the provocation was enough to have made a reasonable person, *of the same age as the defendant and in the same circumstances*, do as he did. (ibid., emphasis added)

When the case was referred for comment to the House of Lords, the trend was taken a little further, with the explicit ruling that the 'reasonable man' against whose hypothetical response that of the defendant was to be measured, was a person of the same age *and sex* as the defendant. In explaining this ruling, the various speakers made it clear that the need for this additional ruling was that sex, like age, 'affected temperament as well as physique', and that what might not reasonably be counted as provocation when directed at one sex might reasonably be regarded as such if directed at the other:

> So, although this has never yet been a subject of decision, a jury could ... take the sex of the accused into account in deciding what might reasonably cause her to lose her self-control. A 'reasonable woman' with her sex eliminated is altogether too abstract a notion for my comprehension, or, I am confident, for that of any jury ... (I)t hardly makes sense to say ... that a normal woman must be notionally stripped of her femininity before she qualifies as a reasonable woman.
>
> ... If words of grievous insult were adressed to a woman, words perhaps reflecting her chastity or her way of life, a consideration of the way in which she reacted would have to take account of how other women, being reasonable women, would or might in like circumstances have reacted.
>
> (*Camplin*, 1978, s All ER 168)

The main effect of this decision was the inclusion of a particular age and sex, congruent with that of the defendant, into the previously invariate reasonable man. The trend is a seemingly progressive one, and consistent with the fashionable principle of individualized treatment. As I shall discuss later, however, the trend has certain more disturbing aspects.

To sum up: legal discourse constructs for itself a standard human subject, endowed with consciousness, reason, foresight, intentionality, an awareness of right and wrong and a knowledge of the law of the land. These are the reasonable attributes which provide the grounds for legal culpability. Yet the law also acknowledges a series of other mental attributes (passions, instincts, unconscious or involuntary impulses, capacities for overwhelming rage or terror) and it concedes the possibility that even in its normal subjects, these might, under certain circumstances, override any rational intentionality, and dominate the subject's behaviour. The 'reasonable man' test allows this 'frailty of the normal' to be acknowledged and taken into account. And the existence of special defences that may be invoked in such cases serves to mark one of the boundaries of the criminal law: behaviours that arise outside of rational consciousness are routinely marginalized from its domain of regulation and sanction. It is this that forms the basis of the defences of duress and automatism, and the partial defence of provocation. Precisely the same forms of reasoning dictate the provisions for subjects whose failings of responsibility are attributed to some specific mental pathology.

Unreasonable subjects

Outside the boundaries of 'normal' subjectivity, the provisions of the criminal law chart a complex terrain of 'pathological' mentality. As will be discussed in later chapters, many of these pathologies are relevant only to the *sentencing* of criminal cases. In limited instances, however, evidence of mental pathology may directly influence the *verdict*. It is this that concerns us here.

Insanity

The rationale of the Insanity defence is contained in the historic M'Naghten Rules,[15] and requires three thing to proven to the satisfaction of the jury:[16]

1. that the defendant was suffering from a 'disease of the mind', (here construed as any mental malfunctioning caused by disease or illness, whether or not of physical origin), at the point when the act was performed;
2. that as a result of this disease, he or she was suffering from a defect of reason;
3. that as a result of this defect of reason he or she either did not know the nature of quality of the act, *or* did not know that it was wrong.[17]

If a court decides that these three criteria are fulfilled, the defendant is regarded as lacking the basic faculties that are necessary for criminal responsibility. He or she therefore must be acquitted of any criminal charge, with a finding of 'not guilty by reason of insanity'. The conceptual narrowness of the defence and its mandatory consequence, (that the defendant is detained in a psychiatric hospital, with release only at the discretion of the Secretary of State), mean that in practice a plea of insanity is very rarely invoked. At the conceptual level, however, it has played a crucial part in the development of medical jurisprudence. Two points about its conception of mental pathology are particularly important for this discussion.

First, it is only concerned with deficiencies of the cognitive faculties of reason and knowledge. It excludes all matters of volition, emotion, or capacity for self-control. The M'Naghten Rules defer unquestioningly to that general legal logic which makes consciousness and rationality the central attributes of criminal responsibility. They therefore provide for the suspension of criminal responsibility only in cases where disease of the mind has so obliterated those attributes that the defendant can scarcely be recognized as a legal subject. As Lord Devlin has suggested:

> As it is a matter of theory, I think there is something logical – it may be astringently logical but it is logical – in selecting as the test of responsibility to the law, reason and reason alone. It is reason which makes a man responsible to the law. It is reason which gives him sovereignty over animate and inanimate things. It is what distinguishes him from the animals, which emotional disorder

does not; it is what makes him man; it is what makes him subject to the law. So it is fitting that nothing other than a defect of reason should give him complete absolution.

(Devlin, 1963, p. 85)

Second, the insanity of the M'Naghten Rules is a legal rather than medical pathology, and certainly cannot be equated with any category of modern psychiatry. It simultaneously excludes the majority of subjects now designated as mentally disordered, (few of whom exhibit such radical disintegration of either consciousness or rationality), and permits the inclusion of a variety of subjects whose abnormal responses are secondary features of ailments such as diabetes or arteriosclerosis[18] which normally are *not* regarded as psychiatric conditions.

The same legal preoccupations ground the related legal provisions which allow certain defendants, (designated 'unfit to plead' or 'under disability in relation to the trail'),[19] to be exempted from trail altogether. The issue in these provisions is not the medical condition or needs of the defendant, but his or her competence to act as a proper legal subject in relation to the trial: to understand the charge and the significance of the plea, to challenge jurors, to instruct counsel, and to follow evidence. If a jury determines, prior to completion of the trial, that the defendant is *not* thus competent, the trial can be foreclosed, and the defendant will be placed in indefinite medical detention on the same terms as a defendant found to be insane. Technically such defendants may be returned to trial in the event of their recovery, but in practice this is rarely if ever done.

Diminished responsibility

Where a person kills or is party to the killing of another, he shall not be convicted of murder if he was suffering from such abnormality of mind (whether arising from a condition of arrested or retarded development of mind or any inherent causes or induced by disease or injury) as substantially impaired his responsibility for his acts and omissions in doing or being a party to the killing ... a person who but for this section would be liable, whether as principle or accessory, to be convicted of murder, shall be liable instead to be convicted of manslaughter.

(Homicide Act, 1957, s 2, (1, 3))

The monolithic logic of the insanity legislation was fractured by the introduction, in 1957, of the doctrine of diminished responsibility for homicide. This legislation provides the conditions for a crucial departure from the exclusive privileging of knowledge and rationality, and instead allows the question of criminal responsibility to be referred to 'the mind's activities in all its aspects':

'Abnormality of mind', which has to be contrasted with the time-honoured expression in the M'Naghten Rules, 'defect of reason' ... appears to be wide enough to cover the mind's activities in all its aspects, not only the perception of physical acts and the ability to form a rational judgment whether an act is right or wrong.

(Byrne, 1960, 3 All ER 1)

Such a definition allows the defence of diminished responsibility to be used in cases involving a strikingly catholic range of 'abnormal' mental states, including those associated with disturbances of emotion, motivation and will power. In the case of 'will power' the interpretation of diminished responsibility has sometimes come close to allowing a defence of 'irresistible impulse' – a notion which English law has elsewhere firmly eschewed. To justify this development, however, a certain precedent may be claimed from the existing legal authority on provocation:

> The ability of the accused to control his physical acts by the exercise of his will was relevant before the passing of the Homicide Act in one case only: that of provocation ... . What is important is that loss of self-control has always been capable of reducing murder to manslaughter, but that the criterion has always been the degree of self-control which would be exercised by a reasonable man, that is to say, a man with a normal mind.
>
> It is against this background of existing law that s 2 (1) of the Homicide Act 1957 falls to be construed ... . 'Abnormality of mind' ... means a state of mind so different from that of ordinary human beings that the reasonable man would term it abnormal ... the expression 'mental responsibility for his acts' points to a consideration of the extent to which the accused's mind is answerable for his physical acts, which must include consideration of the extent of his ability to exercise will power.

(ibid.)

This attempt to assimilate the concept of diminished responsibility to the existing framework of provocation has a paradoxical aspect. The defence of provocation rests on a notion of the *normality* of the mental response that underlies the offence. The defendant is excused because any reasonable subject might have responded in this way, and what is explicitly excluded[20] is recourse to the defence by anyone whose response falls *outside* this norm. In the diminished responsibility provisions, by contrast, a precisely inverted logic is applied. What is invoked is a kind of reverse 'reasonable man' test, in which it is the *abnormality* of the response that grounds the exculpation: the defendant is to be excused in precisely those cases where *no* reasonable person would have responded in such a way.

Whatever their conceptual differences, however, the shared restriction of these defences to cases involving homicide reflects the same practical precedent of giving special attention to the mental state of defendants charged with murder. Current Home Office Standing Orders require that every defendant remanded in custody on a murder charge should initially be admitted to the prison hospital, regardless of whether any mental abnormality is suspected, and that in every such case a pre-trial psychiatric report should be submitted to the court.[21] In part, this practice reflects a legal conception of homicide as an offence particularly likely to be associated with mental disorder. But it is also a product of the unique importance in murder cases of ensuring that any evidence of mental disorder is introduced in relation to the *verdict*, since it will be effectively irrelevant thereafter. For once an offender is convicted of murder, the sentencer has no power of discretion in taking psychiatric factors into account, and at that point, no amount of psychiatric evidence can prevent the imposition of a life sentence. The 1957 legislation and the earlier Infanticide Acts (discussed below) get round this problem by allowing evidence of mental pathology to *prevent* a conviction for murder. In its place is substituted a lesser conviction, which restores to the sentencer a wide range of discretion in the disposal of the case. Pragmatically this is a development which is both expedient and humane, although conceptually it has produced something of a shambles.

Infanticide: imbalance of a mother's mind

The Infanticide Acts[22] antedate the diminished responsibility provisions by several decades. The legislation is effectively similar, however, in that it allows an abnormal mental state that falls short of actual insanity to reduce murder to a lesser offence, on a level with manslaughter. Following the 1957 Act, the majority of infanticide cases could now technically be dealt with under the provisions for diminished responsibility, and it is widely argued that the retention of the special provisions for infanticide is unnecessary.[23] The legislation remains interesting, however, in that it offers an example of certain legal understandings about female mentality and its relationship to the law. The Infanticide Act 1938 provides that:

> Where a woman by any wilful act or omission causes the death of her child, being a child under the age of twelve months, but at the time of the act or omission the balance of her mind was disturbed by reason of her not having fully recovered from the effect of giving birth to the child or by reason of the effect of lactation consequent upon the birth of the child, then, notwithstanding that the circumstances were such that but for this Act the offence would have amounted to murder, she shall be guilty of a felony, to wit of infanticide, and may for such an offence be dealt with and punished as if she had been guilty of the offence of manslaughter of the child.
>
> (Infanticide Act, 1938, s 1)

As a chargeable offence, infanticide is unique in several ways. First, it is the only offence in which mental abnormality is a positive precondition for conviction, (as part of the necessary *mens rea* of the offence), and not, as elsewhere, a defence or partial defence *against* conviction. Infanticide is thus an offence that can *only* be committed by an abnormal subject.[24] Second, the exemption from full responsibility is unique in that it does not seem to depend on the usual logic of criminal responsibility. As the wording stands, the reduction of the offence does not require that killing of the child is actually *related* to the imbalance of mind: it merely has to coincide with it. Finally this legislation is unique in the very obvious links that it makes between female biology and legal pathology. It implies that the normal female conditions of childbirth and lactation are inherently disruptive of the rational subjectivity that the law requires. The notion is of course an old one:

> The operation of the criminal law presupposes in the mind of the person who is acted upon a normal state of strength, reflective power and so on, but a woman after childbirth is so upset, and in such a hysterical state altogether, that it seems to me you cannot deal with her in the same manner as if she was in a regular and proper state of health.
>
> 					(Fitzjames-Stephen, 1873)[25]

This conception of childbirth and lactation as inherently threatening to legal rationality follows the long established tradition which sees woman as the helpless victim of her own biology. And in singling out the killing of a child by its mother as the object for an exclusive legal exemption, the infanticide provision conjures up two mutually contradictory conceptions of the natural morality of maternal attachment. On one hand the logic of exculpation rests on the assumption of a natural maternal tenderness, making a mother's attack on her child almost unthinkable unless arising from some pathology. On the other, it suggests a natural maternal violence, whose origin is in female physiology and whose intensity cannot be subjected to the usual legal restraints governing violence between social subjects.

Sexual division and the subject of the law

It is tempting, of course, to make much of the infanticide provisions. Their interlinking of femininity and psychopathology is so transparent and their presentation of female biology as essentially debilitating to legal subjectivity so accessible. They seem to promise an illustration *par excellence* of the psychiatrization of female crime. Having identified the mechanisms that permit a specific psychiatrization of women within the infanticide legislation, one could carry on to imply that the same mechanisms are necessarily responsible for the disproportionate psychiatrization of women in all the other areas of the law. This strategy of analysis, (which certainly characterizes many of the sociological and historical discussions of women's relationship to the law),[26] allows the argument that the judicial treatment of women is determined by a naturalistic conception of femininity centred on sex and reproduction.

This line of argument is misleading, however. There are actually very few legal provisions which constitute their subjects in such sexually differentiated terms, and they account for little of the sexual discrepancy in the sentencing of male and female offenders. Most of this discrepancy arises in the context of legislation where the law makes no such division by gender and where the issues at stake are quite remote from those of sex and reproduction. In relation to the vast majority of offences, the law formally *refuses* to divide its subjects by gender, as is stated perfunctorily in the Interpretation Act:

In any Act, unless the contrary intention appears,
(a) words importing the masculine gender include the feminine;
(b) words importing the feminine gender include the masculine.

(Interpretation Act, 1978, s 6 a, b)

The atypical instances, where 'the contrary intention' *does* appear, may be engagingly accessible and genuinely interesting, but they are actually peripheral to the legal production of gender differences. The criminal law is quite capable of generating discrepancies of gender without recourse to any 'special' provisions, involving explicitly 'contrary intentions'. The analysis of those cases leaves the important question unanswered: how is it that legal discourse allows sexual divisions to arise so pervasively within the law, despite the stated *neutrality* of the legal subject, and the legislation's declared *indifference* to the gender of legal subjects?

The answer is, in one sense, perfectly simple. The normal centrality of *mens rea* as a necessary component of any offence requires the agents of the law to 'look into the mind' of the defendants whom they judge, and to make their own assessment of what mental state must have accompanied the alleged offence. Legal discourse insists upon the competence of legal agents to perform such assessments, and emphatically refuses any truck with philosophical quibbles about the accessibility of other people's minds:

> So far from saying that you cannot look into a man's mind, you *must* look into it, if you are going to find fraud against him; and unless you think you see what must have been in his mind, you cannot find him guilty.
>
> (*Angus v Clifford*, 1891, QB 22, Ch 449 p. 471)

And in looking into the mind of the defendant, the agents of the law quite routinely – one might almost say inevitably – make commonsense assumptions about human nature and motivation which are powerfully influenced by preconceptions of sexual differences. Common sense tells us that there *are* no ungendered neutral subjects. Whatever the formal injunctions of the law, the defendant whom the court must judge is always an already-gendered man or woman, and in deciding the mental state of the subject, different assumptions about male and female mentality will almost inevitably come into play.

Yet this is not the whole of the story. In addition to underlining the ways in which legal agents do in fact take gender considerations into account when making decisions about legal culpability, I want to make a rather stronger point: that despite its claims to the contrary, judicial discourse actually requires them to do so. This insistence on sexual division occurs, I suggest, deep within judicial discourse, at the heart of its conceptual organization.

In this context, the development of the 'reasonable man test', as discussed above in relation to the Camplin case, offers a graphic illustration of the processes whereby legal discourse constructs its understandings of human normality. It is a far more telling example than that of, say, infanticide, where the importance of gender is made explicit from the start. The various reversals and restatements of the concept of the 'reasonable man' allow one to identify three distinct levels at which assumptions about gender enter the structure of legal discourse.

The most glaring of these, that of the explicit sexualization of a particular legal procedure, is perhaps also the least important. These cases establish a specific set of contexts in which the 'contrary intention appears' and the sex of the accused may explicitly enter the assessment of guilt. In effect, there are two alternative procedures on offer: one in which all defendants are to be assessed by the same standard, (apparently that of the normal adult male), and another in which a variable standard is to be used, reflecting the personal characteristics of the accused, including gender. In these judgments the second proposal is accepted and established by fiat. Of itself this decision is interesting but relatively local and superficial: the ruling could be reversed at some later date without substantially modifying the legal field as a whole. I suggest that it is at this same relatively superficial level of the legal discourse that one can place each of the specific provisions which explicitly differentiate between male and female subjects.

At a deeper level than this, however, one can trace in this series of cases the intrication of assumptions about gender difference into the very *logic* of legal discourse. These rulings rehearse certain old and unresolved questions about the nature of justice itself: faced by human diversity, does justice inhere in judging similar behaviours alike, or in taking account of human differences between the perpetrators?[27] In the particular case under discussion, the argument is basically concerned with age rather than gender, but the category of sexual division is slipped in at the same time, apparently gratuitously, as providing the universal instance of built-in human disparity. It must be right, the argument proposes, to make allowances for age, *just as it is right to make allowance for sex*. The rightness of making allowance for sex is presented as the self-evident case, requiring no demonstration,[28] which is then used to justify, on grounds of analogy, the disputed case of age. Sexual division is here taken as a fundamental apriori of legal reasoning; it structures the legal argument, not simply at the level of the description of particular legal subjects, but at the abstract level of the legal logic itself.

Legal discourse thus incorporates a sexual division not only into what the law can legitimately 'do', in terms of particular provisions and procedures, but also, more profoundly, into what it can reasonably *argue*. Yet beneath even this we can trace a third and yet deeper level of sexual division in legal discourse – at the level of what the law can intelligibly *think*. What is revealed in these arguments is that ultimately legal discourse simply cannot *conceive* of a subject in whom gender is not a determining attribute: it cannot *think* such a subject.

This mental block of the law is not simply a product of the incompatibility of such formal neutrality with the taken-for-granted centrality of gender in the everyday social world. For there are numerous points where the injunctions of legal discourse quite happily depart from the taken-for-granted assumptions of everyday reality, and demand conclusions that are counter-intuitive or even unintelligible to everyday reasoning. It thus has no hesitation, for example, in requiring its agents to presume that no child under ten is capable of a wrongful state of mind,[29] or that diabetic low blood sugar is a form of insanity, justifying the indefinite detention of the sufferer in a psychiatric hospital.[30] But at the point where legal discourse is asked to defend its notion of a neutral legal subject, in whom gender need not be taken into account, it seems suddenly to lose the courage of its convictions.

The embarrassment of the law is tortuously clear in the extracts already quoted. Having first stated that the term 'a reasonable man' is to include in principle 'a reasonable woman', the law lord continues by explaining that even though the two are thus covered by the same term, they must necessarily remain conceptually distinct, since the lack of that conceptual division is literally unthinkable, and its loss would make legal discourse seem nonsensical even to itself. In this context he thus attempts to gesture in speech to that which cannot be thought – a reasonable human subject not identified by sex:

> A reasonable woman with her sex eliminated is altogether too abstract a notion for my comprehension, or I am confident, for that of any jury ... . It hardly makes sense to say ... that a normal woman must be notionally stripped of her femininity before she qualifies as a reasonable woman.
>
> (*Camplin*, 1978, 2 All ER 168)

At the very moment when it attempts to establish the neutrality of the legal subject, we discover the limit of the law's capacity to confront and override the shared assumptions of ordinary reality. At this deepest level, legal discourse is bent back, despite itself, to the contingencies of the everyday, and cannot bring forth the ungendered legal subject which it claims as its own.

This study is concerned with the legal involvement of understandings about gender at all of the levels identified here, but particularly this last. All the legal agents whose statements will be recounted in the course of this study are working from contradictory instructions: enjoined by legal discourse to discount the subject's gender from their judgments, and yet invited, simultaneously, to allow for the centrality of gender at the very heart of their judgment, in their interpretation of the subject's mentality and meanings. For undermining all the explicit requirements for male and female to be treated as one, is the legal proviso that in fact male and female subjects neither *should* be constructed in such indifferent terms, since 'sex ... affects temperament as well as physique', nor *can* be thus constructed, since a 'woman with her sex eliminated is altogether too abstract a notion' for anyone to grasp.

Notes

1 Legal cases are quoted in accordance with standard notation, and these references are italicized throughout the text, to distinguish them from other published works.
2 See Law Commission, 1978. Crimes of 'strict liability', in which subject may be held responsible even if unaware of the offence, are an exception here. These cases are few in number, and generally of minor significance.
3 Cross and Jones (1980, p. 41).
4 See Williams (1978, p. 68f).
5 This provision overturned the previous and much criticized precedent, which made it an irrebuttable presumption of the law that a person foresaw and intended the natural consequences of his acts. (*Smith 1961, AC 290, 1960, 3 All ER 161*).
6 Numerous related permutations are discussed in the legal texts. See, for example, Smith and Hogan (1978, Chapters 2–4).
7 Quoted in Smith and Hogan (1978, p. 39).
8 See *Bratty, 1962, 46 Cr App R1*.
9 See Law Commission, 1977, para 2. 15f.
10 *Hudson and Taylor, 1971, 2 All ER 244*.
11 *Duffy, 1949, 1 All ER, 932*.
12 *Mancini, 1942, 3 All ER, 272*.
13 e.g. *Hudson and Taylor, 1971, 12 All ER, 272*.
14 The Crown Court ruling is cited in the Appeal Court ruling, viz. *Camplin, 1978, 1 All ER 1236*.
15 See Moran (1982), and Walker (1968), for a detailed discussion of this case and of its wide significance for the subsequent jurisprudence of mental disorder.
16 These rules are based closely on answers given by the Judges of the Queen's Bench to a series of legal and jurisprudential questions that were raised by the M'Naghten case. See *M'Naghten 1843, 10 C & Fin 200; 1843–60 All ER Rep 229*.
17 'Wrong' in this context has been taken to mean either morally wrong, or wrong according to the law; the distinction is still disputed.
18 e.g. *Quick, 1973, QB 910* (diabetes) and *Kemp, 1957, 1QB 399* (arteriosclerotic disorder).
19 The latter wording is proposed in the Butler Report (Butler 1975), and has been widely though not uniformly adopted.
20 *Mancini, 1943, 3 All ER, 272* provides the explicit statement of this principle.
21 Home Office Standing Orders, 1981/184.
22 The Infanticide Act 1922; The Infanticide Act 1938.
23 The Butler Report (Butler 1975) recommended the phasing out of infanticide on precisely these grounds. The Criminal Law Revision Committee, however, argued that the infanticide legislation carries the important benefit of avoiding the necessity of initially charging the subject with murder, as must be done in diminished responsibility cases; (Criminal Law Revision Committee Offences Against the Person, Working Paper 26).
24 A curious consequence of this is that if a jury found a woman charged with infanticide to have killed her child whilst mentally *normal*, or whilst disordered due to some other condition, they would technically be required to acquit her, as lacking the necessary *mens rea* for the offence.
25 Quoted in Sachs and Hoff-Wilson (1978, p. 140).

26 e.g. Smith (1981, chapter 7); Edwards (1981, 1985).

27 Ultimately English Law attempts a subtle middle course between these two options, by declaring the principle that like cases should be treated alike, but allowing the characteristics of the subject to influence whether two cases are actually 'alike'. This notion is expressed in the legal formula 'Si duo idem faciunt, non est idem': 'If two people do the same thing, it is not the same thing'.

28 See Glaisdale, L.J. in *Camplin, 1978, 2 All ER 168*: 'This distinction is arguably justified by the implication of the 'reasonable woman' as standard .... [T]he law, in distinguishing something universal like age was doing no more than it had already done in distinguishing implicitly something universal like sex'.

29 Regardless of any evidence, the child under ten is presumed to be mentally 'Doli incapax'. 'Incapable of crime', and thus cannot be convicted of any offence.

30 e.g. in *Quick, 1973, QB 910*, the House of Lords admitted that 'it might be felt to be an affront to common sense' to regard such a person as insane – but none the less insisted that in law the finding was correct.

Chapter three:

No offence intended

The conception of a criminal offence as combining a wrongful deed, (the *actus reus*), and a wrongful mind, (the *mens rea*), establishes for the court a problematic of *human agency*. This chapter examines the evident differences in the way this relation is constructed for male and female cases – differences that have major implications for the assessments of mental abnormality upon which each of the psychiatric verdicts depends.

As already described, homicide is an area in which psychological considerations are given a particular importance in relation to the verdict, where they must be addressed with particular care and attention by the agents of criminal justice, and where psychiatric advice and evidence is routinely sought. It is also an area where psychiatric disposals are unusually common. It is for these reasons that I have based this part of the analysis on cases involving this group of offences.

The precise selection of cases and material is described in Appendix B. Briefly, the cases include all the female and an equal number of randomly selected male homicides appearing before a single Crown Court over a two-year period.[1] The materials discussed are drawn from the court files on these cases, and include psychiatric and social enquiry reports, the written statements of the police, and documents relating to the defence and court procedure. The analysis of these documents demonstrates the different routes along which the assessments of male and female mentality typically proceed, and indicates how this influences the possibility of a special psychiatric verdict. As I shall discuss in later chapters, these differences in the construction of male and female cases are also of relevance in understanding the choice of *sentence*, even in cases where only a standard conviction is made.

Female minds: intense, complex, tangled

> At this stage it is difficult to untangle the complexities of her emotional state at the time. Although she now presents as emotionally flattened, there is no doubt that the killing took place in a context of intense psychological pressure, culminating in a transient loss of control. I could not say that she was fully responsible for her acts and omissions on the night of the offence.
>
> (Psychiatric report, case 10, female accused of murder)

In comparing the treatment of psychological issues in these documents, one of the most striking differences is a purely quantitative one. In all the documents, whether produced by doctors, probation officers, the police or lawyers, there is simply *more* about the mental life of women. There are more references to feelings, more attention to psychological responses and more narration of thought. Such references are not *absent* from the documentation of male cases, but they are certainly less central and less meticulously traced.

The observation of a quantitative difference is not simply impressionistic. Calculating a frequency of references to mental life (albeit rather crudely) as a ratio of statements that do mention some psychological process to those that do not, one finds the frequency almost twice as great in female texts as male. And in absolute terms, (since more reports tend to be prepared for each female case, and each of these texts tends to be longer overall than the male ones), there are on average three times as many statements touching on these issues in the documentation of female cases. Taken together, the psychiatric and social enquiry reports in this sample provided the court with an average of fifty-five lines of text relating to the mental life of each female defendant, and an average of eighteen lines in the male cases. Indeed, whereas *all* the female reports contain at least a desultory documentation of various aspects of their inner experiences, many of the male reports hardly mention such matters at all. Surprisingly, this is particularly common amongst psychiatric reports, where one might have expected the most explicit consideration of the defendant's mind.

What follows, for example, is the full text of the psychiatric report on a man charged with murder. Along with a female co-defendant, this man had clubbed and hacked to death, (using various items of kitchen equipment ranging from frying pan to carving knife), a casual acquaintance who had invited them to his house. They had subsequently set light to the body and departed, taking various items of apparently inconsequential booty: old clothes, an electric kettle, a plastic shopping bag ... I have italicized those parts which I interpret as references to his mental life.

> I have interviewed this man, read the statements relating to the present charge, and received a communication from the Probation and After-care Service regarding a previous period of probationary supervision.

Alan Baker was born in B and brought up in C. There is no family history of criminality, alcoholism or mental disorder, and he has lost contact with his only sibling, a sister. He worked in unskilled occupations before joining the Navy at the age of seventeen years, where he served for eight years. Since leaving the Navy, Baker has lived in C, where he has been employed in the building trade as a driver.

Alan Baker married first at the age of nineteen years, and there are three children by the relationship. He married again eight years ago, and his second wife has seven children by a previous relationship. There are problems in the marriage, and Baker periodically leaves home when he engages in drinking binges. He came to London five weeks before his arrest on the current charge, and he lived in the D area, and worked on a casual basis as a driver.

The defendant is *of average intelligence*. I could elicit *no evidence of mental disorder and he is fit to plead*. He had consumed a good deal of alcohol on the day of the alleged offence, but he was an habitual drinker, and there was *no evidence of psychosis*.

(Psychiatric report, case 66, male accused of murder and arson; italics added)

The mental life of the defendant is referred to only negatively, as an absence of anything worthy of report. His intelligence is normal; he is fit to plead; there is no evidence of disorder or psychosis. There is no attempt to substantiate or elaborate these findings by reference to any positive observations of his mental state; no attempt to explicate his feelings, perceptions, attitudes or thoughts; no indication of any psychological factor that might have determined, influenced, or even been relevant to the shocking offence with which he is charged. One is given the impression of a human being with no inner life at all.

The treatment of his female co-defendant is very different. Two psychiatric reports were prepared in her case, each running to four pages of text and including detailed reflections on her mental make-up and feelings, as well as intimate information about her biography. These texts are too long to be reproduced in full, but the following extracts illustrate their characteristic features. Again, as throughout this section, I have italicized the references to the subject's mental state:

PERSONALITY: ... Carol Dobson, a woman with *no particular aims or interests in life* says she is not a violent person. She freely admits a lesbian sexual orientation, which was present even at junior school. Unable to confide in her mother, she *hated* living at home, and throughout her life has *experienced the sense of isolation* which so often accompanies such a condition ....

MENTAL STATE IN CUSTODY: The defendant was received into custody on the 28th April, and on the 30th April was described by the prison medical officer as *cheerful, bewildered and not depressed*. She was sleeping well, and her appetite was good. During May she complained of headaches which were thought to be due to *nervous tension*, and in June she continued to *feel rather uptight* ....

PRESENT MENTAL STATE: ... Throughout the interview Carol's manner was polite and affable, and she was *not unduly depressed*, bearing in mind the circumstances she now finds herself in. Her *memory appeared entirely normal, and her thought processes rational*.

OPINION: (1) She is *fit to plead*. (2) She has *no mental illness* but her history of alcoholism, and irregular and anti-social behaviour, in conjunction with her problems with her homosexuality and transvestism, clearly label her as a *psychopathic personality disorder*, probably as a result of childhood deprivation, in conjunction with *low intelligence*. As a result she should be regarded as *possibly not fully in control of herself when upset* …. (3) At the material time, although her responsibility for her actions or omissions was not in my view substantially diminished, it may have been diminished to the extent that she *did not intend* to kill her alleged victim.
(Psychiatric report, case 3, female accused of murder and arson; italics added)

The difference in length of these two reports could be said to exaggerate their difference in content. Even in reports of comparable length, however, the same differences remain marked. Statements about the lives and mentalities of female defendants tend to be elaborated by reference to the *internal* significance of the matters described; depth and texture are provided by the interweaving of parallel commentaries on these women's inner feelings and outward lives. In reports concerning male defendants, the elaboration of information is achieved more characteristically through an accretion of purely *external* detail. Compare, for example, the following two passages, both of which refer to disfiguring injuries received by the defendant during childhood. In the first case, the defendant had been injured in a road accident when aged five:

Elaine was badly concussed and cut about the face … from that period she *suffered from constant nightmares and exhibited deeply disturbed* behaviour …. She had a bad time at school where she was called 'scarface' and other nicknames … and her mother felt that all this accounted for her *very quiet, withdrawn and solitary nature*, and her *ability to lose herself in daydreams* …. After a series of successful [plastic surgery] operations in 1975, she *appeared to gain confidence* …
(Social Enquiry Report, case 19, female accused of murder; italics added)

A direct link is drawn between the concrete damage to the defendant's body, and her psychological responses and development. In the next case, however, no such interweaving of the internal and external worlds of the defendant is attempted:

Frank's childhood was marred only by his injury, in a fire, when he was three years old. He was very badly scarred, mostly on his arms. He spent six months in hospital after this accident, and his childhood was punctuated by readmissions to hospital for continuing treatment. He underwent extensive plastic surgery as recently as 1981, and he awaits further operations …. If any criticism is to be made of his upbringing, it would have to be on the grounds that he may have been somewhat over-indulged. Frank's mother blamed herself for the accident – a reaction that is as normal as it was unfounded. It is not surprising that she should have sought to compensate her son for his *suffering*, though he may have been ill-served by this.
(Psychiatric report, case 70, male accused of manslaughter; italics added)

No mention is made of the defendant's own reaction to injury (although his *mother's* emotional reaction is treated as significant). As far as the defendant himself is concerned, the significance of the injury is seen to lie only in its external repercussions: the operations, the hospital admissions; the maternal over-indulgence.

It might be supposed that this difference simply reflects 'what is there'. Women are commonly believed to be more sensitive and emotional than men, and more ready to express their feelings. Consequently it would not be surprising to find differences in what they say to the professional agents who compile these reports. And reading through the documents it is easy to find examples of female defendants who have been manifestly emotional in the course of the assessment interviews, and of males who have gone through the process without any such expression:

> ... a rather taciturn lad and less than cooperative at interview .... He does not appear to be bothered about the prospect of a long prison sentence or about the death of the victim, but gives an adequate account of the offence .... A delinquent youth ... no evidence of mental illness, subnormality or psychopathy.
>
> (Psychiatric report, case 78, male accused of murder)

As typical in male cases, the comments are perfunctory, and offer no psychological illumination of the case. Perhaps the defendant has said nothing to suggest any internal world. Perhaps there is nothing to say. But compare this with the vividly psychological portrayal of the following defendant, who appears in material terms to have been equally inexpressive:

> During my conversation with Miss Grant, I have found her to be *divorced from the emotional context* of her conversation .... She does not let people get close to her and *is inclined to suppress her feelings*. [She is] an *isolated repressed woman*, who clearly has *difficulty in facing the reality of her situation*. Professional counselling may help Miss Grant to improve her abilitiy in making friendships and develop self-expression. Certain aspects of her *personality* and needs may be explored, with a resultant increase of *insight* in her functioning as a person.
>
> (Social Enquiry Report, case 8, female accused of murder; italics added)

In female cases, any expression of feelings is recorded as confirmation of the woman's inner life. And the absence of such expression is *also* recorded – not as indicating any *absence* of inner life, but as evidence of its existence in a particular and pathological form, suppressed, repressed, divorced from itself. A female subject whose subjectivity is not, somewhere, in some way, characterized by an intense inner life seems almost unthinkable.

Male lives: in on the action

Equally revealing are the differences in the treatment of men and women's external behaviour. In the male cases, one seems to move on to firmer ground at this point: we get a much clearer impression of their material involvement in the world than of their mentality. The following, for example, is the psychiatric report on a young man who had killed the child of his common-law wife. I apologize in advance for the flatness of this biographical catalogue – though it is precisely this quality that I wish to illustrate.

This man is charged with murder. I have read the depositions. I examined him on 9th February. I asked him to give me an account of the events leading to his arrest. He said 'well, when I come home from work, my bird said "he won't go out and play". So I bounced him on the bed and took him in the front room. He went dizzy, and I gave him a drink of water. Next night I came home from the gym (I was doing community service for robbery) and he was dead'.

FAMILY HISTORY: The accused was born in B and has lived in London all his life. His father is aged forty-eight and is a foreman painter and decorator. Asked about his relationship with his father he said 'OK, fine'. As a child he was not punished much, nor did he undergo any privations. His father apparently is a moderate drinker and has a clean police record. His mother is aged forty-five and works as a cook in a school. With her he also gets on 'fine'. She has an occasional drink with the father at weekends. The accused is the middle of three brothers. The elder is aged twenty-two, and is unemployed and has served a prison sentence. The younger brother, aged nineteen, is an electrician and has never been in police trouble.

Previous personal history:

EDUCATION: The accused attended a catholic comprehensive school in B to the age of sixteen. He was not a good scholar but is literate. He played truant frequently for one and a half years towards the end of his schooldays. Asked what he did when he was playing truant, he said 'I'd just muck about and go to the parks'. At school he played badminton and did some weightlifting.

OCCUPATIONS: He attended a training course in C. He said 'I've had lots of jobs. I've worked on modernizing houses, doing all sorts of jobs, bricklaying, plastering, labouring, painting and decorating. I'd be classed as a labourer'. He said that his average earnings were £60 a week. He has however been unemployed since May or June and lives on the dole, obtaining £120 per two weeks.

PHYSICAL ILLNESS: He fractured his leg at age fourteen in an adventure playground and was admitted to D Hospital. Otherwise he has kept in good physical health.

PSYCHIATRIC HISTORY: He has never been examined by a psychiatrist previously, and I can find nothing of note in this context. He told me at one stage that he was not a member of the National Front or the 'Skinheads', although he has the appropriate hairdo. He also denied that he had a bad temper, and insisted that he had no intention of doing the victim any harm. He did go on to say that when he was about sixteen or seventeen years old he was involved in fights, but has since quietened down.

HABITS: Alcohol – he goes out drinking on Friday nights in pubs with his pals. He has on these occasions about five or six pints. He maintains that he is not an alcoholic. He smokes about fifteen cigarettes a day, and denies the use of illicit drugs.

SEXUAL HISTORY: He first had sexual intercourse at the age of thirteen or fourteen with local girls of the same age. He maintains that he was engaged about two years ago, but the relationship broke up. He began to cohabit with his current girlfriend (the mother of the victim) in December last year, first in a squat in E from which they were evicted. From there they moved to another squat in F and have lived there since September. His cohabitee is twenty-three years old and has two children including the victim. He insists that his relationship with his girlfriend is 'fine' and that he got on very well with her two children. He says that he and his cohabitee and her two children lived on his dole money and her child allowance as a family.

CRIMINAL COURT: At the age of fifteen or sixteen he was charged with stealing milk from a doorstep and was cautioned. Also at the age of sixteen he was 'nicked in a stolen car' and fined. At the age of nineteen he was arrested for drunken driving on his mate's motor cycle. He was fined and banned for eighteen months. Then at the age of nineteen he was involved in a robbery of a taxi driver with two of his mates. The were caught by other taxi drivers and the accused was eventually given two hundred hours community service, working in a gym putting up apparatus.

On examination he presented as a slightly built young man in good physical health with a skinhead hairdo. He had professional tattoos on both arms, with a few amateur ones. He wore an earring in his left ear.

He was of dull normal intelligence but was cooperative throughout. There was no evidence of mental disorder.

OPINION: This man is not suffering from any form of mental disorder. I have therefore no recommendation to make. He is fit to plead, to stand his trial and to suffer any penalty the court may award.

(Psychiatric report, case 61, male accused of murder)

Here we have a person, an identity, but the only 'personal' details are literally only skin deep: the hairdo and the tattoos mark a boundary beyond which the report makes no attempt to go. This individual is a subject of *action*: his individuality is marked out by what he *does*, where he *participates*, how he *acts* in the world. The reporter finds all that need be said about him in the domains of the active and external: his occupations, his finances, his habits, his sexual activities, his crimes and so on. This treatment is characteristic of the documentation of male cases.

Female cases receive a quite different gloss. Somehow female subjects are never quite accorded this domain of action. At the simplest level, there is a straightforward paucity of statements which even relate to women's action. Any material narrative in these reports tends to focus, not on what these women *do*, but on what *happens* to them. Indeed, the documents tend to undermine the sense of these women doing anything at all, by presenting them as perpetually moved by others' agency rather than their own. They are dominated and dependent; they are victims of circumstance. The following, for example, comes from a report on a woman who killed her lodger when he refused to eat his supper; she threw a gallon of paraffin over him, followed by a lighted match:

It would be hard to overestimate the effect which these events [i.e. the killing] have had upon Mrs Harris. She is naturally, I think, a somewhat nervous and anxious person, and at times has felt quite overwhelmed by her feelings of guilt. As she has told me her history, I have felt the stage being set for this tragedy by her parents. Unloved and repressed by them, she has found herself in relationships which seem to have reinforced her feelings of worthlessness and uselessness. From her description, both her second husband and the victim seem to have been violent borderline alcoholics, and for much of her life she appears to have been the one who has been put upon and generally exploited, until this violent retaliation took place.

(Social Enquiry Report, case 7, female accused of murder)

The woman does not act of her own volition: she is a puppet of others who 'set the stage for her tragedy'. She does not *make* relationships, but merely 'finds herself' in them, exploited, put upon and victimized. And even the killing is not presented as an act that she herself has done, but simply as a 'retaliation' that 'takes place' (causing her terrible distress in the process). The activity of the woman is allowed to vanish; what she 'does' is effortlessly assimilated to what 'happens'.

Between mind and body

What is missing in these cases [of automatism] appears to most people as a vital link between mind and body; and both the ordinary man and the lawyer might well insist on this by saying that in these cases there is not 'really' a human action at all, and certainly nothing for which anyone should be made criminally responsible.

(Hart, op. cit.)[2]

The two previous sections of this chapter demonstrate differences between male and female cases in the description of both experience and behaviour. But there is also a further issue at stake. As is indicated by Hart in the passage above, the legal conception of criminal responsibility depends not only on the coexistence of mind and body, but also on a vital link *between* them. The effective obliteration of this link in the construction of female cases is only the terminal stage of the process that I have been describing throughout.

From experience to action

In the ideal and 'normal' case, the conceptual distinction between the behaviour and the mentality of the criminal subject (the *actus reus* and *mens rea* of the offence) are for all practical purposes reunified. In the absence of evidence to the contrary, the wrongful deed can be assumed to be simply the concrete expression of a wrongful mind, whose natural presence behind the deed can be simply 'read off' from the surface of the subject's behaviour.

This conception meshes quite happily with the construction of male cases.

Their frequent silence on psychological matters can be read as simply an absence of 'evidence to the contrary'. And when references *are* made to the mental life of males, they are typically in a form consistent with this expectation of a normal and causal relation between mentality and action. They are generally straightforward statements of rational motivation; they are typically in the form 'x was in his mind and so he did y':

> Employment: YOP scheme: worked as a shelf filler, local supermarket . *Left because he felt underpaid.* Warehouse in B, labourer. *Left through boredom.*
> (Police document, case 70, male accused of manslaughter; italics added)

> When the deceased saw how much blood there was on him and saw that Ivan was responsible, the deceased [Ivan's father], attacked Ivan afresh .... Ivan *was very frightened, realized that his father would kill him if could, and therefore* used every means at his disposal to kill his father in self-defence.
> (Psychiatric report, case 86, male accused of murder; italics added)

Reports on women present a quite different picture. Despite the rich elaboration of what these women think and feel, it is rare for these feelings to appear as the motive or cause of any action. The typical form of statement places the subject in a purely passive position: 'y happened to her and so she felt x'. Statements which present inner states as motives for action (which made up a large proportion of the psychological statements in male cases) appear only half as often in the documents relating to female cases.[3] And where such statments do appear, this motivation to action is almost invariably presented in pathological terms:

> None of her relationships has endured, and it is possible to infer that *the nature of her emotional needs makes her prone to making an unwise choice of partner.*
> (Psychiatric report, case 16, female accused of murder; italics added)

> She began to be suspicious that her husband was having an extramarital relationship .... This naturally distressed her very considerably and *she took a slight overdose because of this distress.*
> (Psychiatric report, case 9, female accused of murder; italics added)

There was a similar pattern of sexual differentiation in the interviews between defendants and the police.[4] With male suspects, there was never any specific interrogation as to the psychological determinants of the suspect's behaviour, other than a direct 'Why did you do it?'. Their recorded enquiries in male cases were almost exclusively confined to the establishment of material facts, and the origin of the suspect's behaviour in normal conscious intentions appears in the majority of cases to be simply taken for granted.[5] In interviewing females on the other hand, the subjects' motivation is treated as a matter for definite investigation, and police officers are quick to look for pathological explanations. In several of the interviews, police officers ask female suspects if they had been upset or depressed at the time of the offence; sometimes they simply suggest a psychological explanation for the offence, and invite the woman to endorse it:

POLICE OFFICER: Can you remember last night *feeling desperately angry because of all this abuse you had suffered over the years?*
SUSPECT: When Jack and me rowed I often said, look Jack you have dragged a lot of things out of me over the years and we are getting too old for it.
POLICE OFFICER: *Are you conscious of the fact that possibly last night the whole matter came to a head and you had to do something to stop him?*
SUSPECT: I don't know how I feel. I know at times I really felt hatred when he started on me, but never to the point I wanted to kill him.

(Police Record of Interview, case 11,
female awaiting charge for homicide; italics added)

Reversal and dissolution

In these respects, women subjects are typically treated differently from the normal subjects of the law. Their behaviours are not 'in the absence of evidence to the contrary' assumed to be simply the external face of rational intentions. Instead, what is frequently assumed is a tortuous mediation or absolute dissolution of the relationship between mentality and behaviour. In the first of these cases, the female subject is presented as being driven from outside. Her inner experiences merely mediate between the external conditions that propel her and the behaviours which she is driven to perform:

[Whilst in custody] she is reported to have lost her temper because she could not get a pen to write to her mother and as a result she damaged her locker and a light fitting .... Personality assessment showed .... that she reacted strongly to emotionally arousing situations.

(Psychiatric Reports, case 1, female accused of murder)

In these cases, the subject's behaviour seems more 'caused' than 'intended', but at least there does seem to be *some* notion of mental agency involved. Equally commonly, however, women's behaviour is presented as somehow divorced from any agency at all. Behaviour and inner experience may be documented in parallel, but any connection between the two is discounted or denied: behind the behaviour itself there is only an absence, a disconnection, a failure of experience. Sometimes this absence is stated only as a retrospective amnesia for the events in question. More important, however, are those cases where the absence of experience is presented as simultaneous with the event. Here it is not simply a disruption of the subsequent recounting of a relationship between behaviour and intentionality, but an absence of this relationship itself: the woman did not intend her deed, did not know or understand that she was doing it, experienced nothing in relation to it. In nine of the twenty-five female homicides,[6] it is accepted that the women concerned have stabbed their victim through the heart or lungs 'without intending any serious harm'; in one novel case we are even told that a woman who has forcibly put a plastic bag over her girlfriend's head and tied it on with an electric flex may not have been aware that she was thereby killing her.[7]

The following case is interesting in that it openly theorizes this absence of experience. The woman has broken into the family home of her lover, where she has a fight with her lover's wife and kills her. She then sets fire to the house, which results in the additional death her lover's two children.

> Karis remembers the early parts of the fight except that she does not remember having her hair pulled out. Her mind is then quite blank until she realized that [the wife] had stopped struggling and was seriously wounded. This fact can easily be explained by Karis becoming totally involved in the battle and oblivious to everything around her. She was brought back to her senses, she states, by the sound of one of the children crying. She notes that a fire had been started in the room, but she does not remember starting it. In a daze she fed the child and left the house .... Her lack of memory for these events can be explained by her natural defences in protecting herself from the consequences of her actions .... I do not think it at all likely that she planned to commit this crime. The crime in all probability developed from the original fight, and the tragic events which followed were caused by Karis's dissociation from her own feelings, so that she was in an emotionless trance and unable to appreciate what she had done, or take steps to prevent a further tragedy from occurring. At this point she could not make responsible decisions. This too was her natural defence against extreme stress. It is a well known and typical hysterical reaction.
>
> (Psychiatric report, case 6, female accused of murder,
> manslaughter × 2 and arson)

We are offered a series of disjunctions, absences, dissociations. The woman is oblivious to everything around her; she does not know what injuries she is causing or sustaining; she is in a daze, in a trance, dissociated from her feelings. Across the whole drama there is an absence of intention, of will, of responsibility for action. By an accretion of small strokes the report erases her agency; the crime merely 'develops'; the tragic events 'follow'; a further tragedy 'occurs'.

It is all presented in psychological terms, using loosely psychodynamic vocabulary. The reference to unconscious processes – defences, dissociation, hysteria – seems at first to promise the reassertion of *some* kind of agency, even if constructed in quite different terms from that rational conscious intentionality demanded by the law. On closer examination, however, one discovers that the text stops short of even this. The notion of the unconscious that is implicitly invoked here is not used to explain the emergence of behaviour, but only to provide a gloss for the disappearance of her experience. The woman's defences, dissociation and hysteria are not presented as the origin of any of her actions; they are merely the sink into which her consciousness and understanding seem to drain and disappear.

Shifting the responsibility

These documents typically construct male cases in the terms of action and intentionality which the doctrine of criminal responsibility would seem to require, but they construct their female cases quite differently. This difference is to some extent reflected in the distribution of verdicts. Numerically, the pattern of verdicts amongst my fifty cases, (described fully in Appendix B), is much as might be expected on the basis of the national figures. Of the twenty-four male and twenty-two female cases that result in a conviction, there were three male and six female cases where psychiatric evidence led to a reduction of a murder charge to manslaughter by reason of diminished responsibility, and a further three cases where women were convicted of infanticide rather than murder, on grounds of mental imbalance consequent upon the birth. One women, who had strangled her mother, was found unfit to plead. Overall, a verdict specifically dependent upon psychiatric factors was thus made in ten female and three male cases.

The sexual bias seems clear, and my general discussion of the construction of male and female cases indicates some of the overall differences that underlie this bias. But my discussion so far will not explain why only some and not *all* of the female subjects were exempted from responsibility, or how any of the males achieved a psychiatric verdict at all. It is therefore necessary to turn back to these specifically 'psychiatric' cases, and ask what it is about their construction that differentiates them from the others.

Male irresponsibility: the madman and the monster

In the male cases,[8] all of diminished responsibility, this can be done fairly easily. They are all constructed in terms that are strikingly different from the other male cases; indeed, almost all the generalizations about male cases which I have made above can be reversed in relation to these three anomalous instances. The appearance of 'uncharacteristic' features in all these 'abnormal' male cases is illustrated in the following report, which concerns a man who has killed his ex-wife, a prostitute. Prior to the killing he had for some time been living a fugitive life with their son, whose custody was in dispute.

Mr Lawson described the environment in which he was raised with great bitterness .... His urgent desire to have a stable family background seemed uppermost in his mind throughout his life, and played no small part in the tragedy that ensued ....

He met his wife first of all when she was a child of eleven, and his relationship with her was bizarre. Eventually it became a sexual relationship .... He seems vulnerable in the context of the loss of security and affection .... It would seem impossible to exaggerate the trauma which he suffered emotionally at the hands of this unstable, irresponsible and totally amoral wife. None the less, it is evident that he was besotted with her .... As a result of her behaviour he reacted with depression ....

To come back to the events leading up to the tragedy: and it is a story that lends weight to the old adage that truth is stranger than fiction. It is important to go back to the time when on impulse he had taken his son out of the country and out of the clutches of his wife .... Having arrived [abroad] with his young child he felt so forlorn that he sat in the ariport and wept ....

He describes in vivid and poignant terms his experience [after his deportation back to London], when he was forcibly separated from his son at the police station .... Mr Lawson was suffering from an anxiety depressive state of very considerable severity. His mental illness was the result of the long period of tension and anxiety occasioned by his life as a virtual fugitive .... The acute symptoms arose when he was finally faced with deportation, and from then on there was a rapid build up of emotional tension leading finally to an emotional state in which he became not only acutely depressed, anxious and agitated, but also confused. Eventually he was determined to destroy himself, but instead he turned the knife on his wife. The frenzied killing appears to have all the hall-marks of a crime of passion, i.e. a volcanic eruption of pent-up emotion ....

I believe that a plea of diminished responsibility could be substantiated in that at the time of the killing he was suffering from such abnormality of mind, i.e. mental illness (anxiety depressive state) due to disease of the mind as substantially impaired his mental responsibility for his acts .... However on this present showing I do not think that further medical treatment is indicated, and I have therefore no medical recommendation to make. He is fit to plead.

(Psychiatric Report, case 81, male accused of murder)

The case is starkly dissimilar to the other male cases. The defendant's behaviour is at no point treated as self-explanatory, but always as the product of a tortured and tortuous mentality. He is a subject severed from rational intentionality, who responds with passionate intensity to all the impacts of external pressures. Childhood events have dangerously flawed his personality, and the events of adulthood have left him catastrophically traumatized. His intentions are constantly abnormal in form and unpredictable in operation; his motivations are always overwhelming. His crime is a 'volcanic eruption of pent-up emotion', in which the relation between his intentions and his behaviour is anything but straightforward:

Eventually he determined to kill himself, but instead he turned the knife upon his wife.

(Ibid.)

Certain parallels can obviously be drawn between the characteristics of this text and those concerning women. As in female cases, there is an emphasis on inner experience, a denial of intent, an emphasis on emotional attachments and a readiness to displace responsibility on to others, including the victim. Yet despite these similarities, it would be misleading to argue that the special construction of the male 'psychiatric' case is simply the same as the routine construction of female ones. For there remains something jarringly different about this text.

Most simply, it shocks. The events and circumstances are presented as an outrageous breach of everything that is normal and natural. The crime is the product of a set of historical and personal contingencies that are monstrous, singular and bizarre. The importance of this observation may not be immediately apparent – for are not the female cases *also* shocking, *also* outrageous? Certainly one can stand at a certain critical distance from some of them, and reconstruct their events as equally monstrous. But their narratives are not actually presented in this way. In female cases, the same structural characteristics are used to quite different effect.

In the case above, for example the term 'tragedy' is not used in its bland and popular sense, (as it is in female cases), to assimilate the crime to some impersonal domain of unfortunate natural events, for which no one in particular is to blame. Instead his case is presented as a 'tragedy' in the purest dramaturgical sense of the term; its pageant of terrible suffering is cathartic, moral, and fearfully human. Stress is laid on the strangeness of the tale to be told ('it is a story that lends weight to the old adage that truth is stranger than fiction'), but none the less the events are presented as the precisely comprehensible outcome of the 'tragic flaws' of the defendant. As an acting subject he is desperately damaged and dangerous, but he is still *absolutely an acting subject*.

Rather the same point may be made about the emphasis on the psychological. In the female cases, the constant references to the defendants' troubled minds are used to embed their crimes in a context of 'natural female experience': emotionality, vulnerability, victimization. The female offender is made to seem *normal*, and any sense of shock at her behaviour is neutralized by the implication that under such circumstances any ordinary woman might have responded in such a way:

POLICE OFFICER: Were you having a period at the time of the offence? ... I understand some women get depressed during their periods, that's why I asked you.
(Police record of interview, case 15, female awaiting charge for murder)

This too was her natural defence against extreme stress. It is a well known and typical hysterical reaction.
(Psychiatric report, case 6, female accused of murder, manslaughter and arson, op. cit)

These conflicts, along with all the usual pressures of caring for a new baby, eventually took their toll.
(Psychiatric report, case 14, female accused of murder and cruelty to a child)

In the male case, on the other hand, the psychologization of the offence is worded to *produce* shock. Stress is laid upon the aberrant and entirely singular nature of the defendant's mental state, portraying it, (as in the classic judicial statement on diminished responsibility),[9] as 'a state of mind so different from that of ordinary human beings that a reasonable man would call it abnormal'.

Much the same points could be made about the other male cases which received a psychiatric verdict. One involved a flamboyantly paranoid schizophrenic, who beheaded his ex-wife and her lover whom he believed to be running the Mafia. The other was a young man diagnosed as a psychopath, who stabbed to death a young woman whilst he was out on a burglary, and then raped her as she died. This later case is interesting in its refusal to allow any displacement of the man's moral responsibility for his crimes, despite the medical diagnosis, and despite the agreement that a plea of diminished responsibility is in order. As in many of the female cases, the medical reports describe a childhood characterized by gross deprivations and concede that he is a desperately 'damaged' individual. Unlike the female cases, however, they at no point equate this with any disruption of agency, or allow the subject's subsequent violence to be laid at anyone else's door: when the defendant himself asserts that his problems are due to 'the system', and that 'society' and his 'experiences' have made him what he is, this is briskly dismissed as self-excusing and treated as reprehensible in itself. All the most shocking of his statements about his feelings (concerning his hatred of society, his enjoyment of violent pornography, his sadistic fantasies) are recounted without question. But each of his attempts to claim emotions which might link him to the common weal of human experience are explicitly rejected:

> He told me that he intended to commit suicide in the near future. However I did not find his mood depressed [and] ... he showed no remorse or other emotions at any time other than being angry and menacing when challenged about whether he was being truthful .... He was self-excusing and said 'society as a whole has pushed me into being what I am'. Although he at times said that he regretted his crimes, he did so without conviction .... Mullen is suffering from a psychopathic disorder. He is indeed the psychopath in pure culture .... He has attempted suicide three times with overdoses. He has abused drugs. He seems incapable of feeling remorse for his crimes and is indeed self-excusing.
> (Psychiatric report, case 80, male accused of murder)

As I noted earlier, where a woman fails to express a 'normal' emotionality, normal emotions are none the less attributed to her, albeit in a repressed and therefore pathological form. Here one can observe the opposite process. Far from 'reading in' any hidden normality beneath the surface of this man's statements, this report deletes from them any claim to normality that they may include: if he is not to be constituted as a totally reasonable, ordinary subject, then he must be converted into a monster.

Female irresponsibility: the pathology of the normal

The differences between the construction of those male 'psychiatric' cases and the other male cases are easy to trace. But what of the female ones? Amongst the female cases, what differentiates those which receive psychiatric verdicts from those which do not? The short and important answer to this question is *very little*.

All those characteristics which serve to detach the female subject from the norm of rational intentionality appear with remarkable uniformity in the documentation of female cases. And this remains the case whether or not any attempt is made to present the defendants in strictly pathological terms, as eligible for a special psychiatric verdict. Consider the case quoted earlier in which the woman kills her lover's wife, sets light to his house, and leaves his children to die in the blaze. In the passage quoted, a vivid account is given of the woman's dissociated state, with all its characteristic absences of understanding, intention and will. The description might almost seem to be directed towards a plea of insanity, on grounds that she either did not know what she was doing, or did not know that it was wrong. At the very least it would seem to imply a finding of diminished responsibility. Not a bit of it. Far from arguing that the woman's responses and experiences are in any way abnormal or pathological, the report insists on their normality. Indeed, instead of asserting any deviation from a state of normality, the report concludes that this defendant is actually *a perfectly normal young woman in every respect*:

> ON EXAMINATION: A pleasant, straightforward girl, speaking good English. Open with good social skills and normal emotions. I could detect no sign of any mental illness or abnormal thought process. She could not be described as having a personality disorder. Her intensity was, however, evident at the interview, and I got the impression that she has a definite breaking point, and cannot tolerate events beyond this. She suffers from migraine and when younger suffered from premenstrual tension. However at the time the crime with which she is charged was committed, she was on the contraceptive pill and tension-free, so this is not a factor ….
>
> SUMMARY AND OPINION: I have carefully examined this defendant and can find no psychiatric reason for her actions. She is a perfectly normal young woman in every respect.
>
> (Psychiatric report, case 6, female accused of murder, manslaughter × 2, and arson)

The female subjects of medico-legal discourse are trapped in a series of paradoxes. As I described in the last chapter, legal discourse makes contradictory demands of those judging women: both to ignore their gender and to take it into account. Female offenders, no less than male, are required to be 'reasonable', yet the reasonableness that is to be demanded of them is that of 'normal ordinary women'. And looking at the terms in which women are presented to the courts, it is hard to be sure what kind of reasonableness this might be.

For herein is the second paradox. Those judging women can defer to a concept of femininity that seems to exclude normal women from the standard of rationality that the law routinely assumes. The 'perfectly normal womanhood' of the woman described above seems a very far cry from that rational conscious subject required by the doctrine of criminal responsibility. The construction of the criminal responsibility of normal woman is fractured by an inherent ambiguity.

The same ambiguity characterizes the construction of 'abnormal' female cases. Just as the normal case appears somehow pathological, so the pathological case appears somehow normal. The effect of the psychiatrization of female cases is not, as in male cases, to make the subject into some kind of startling monster. Instead it proceeds through a delicate process of psychological salvage, in which what is demonstrated is not the absence of her (feminine) normality, but its reassuringly familiar presence beneath its aberrant manifestations. This is precisely the *same* path as is taken in the 'normalization' of these cases. It is therefore never clear in advance whether the assertion of a woman's feminine normality will operate to shore up or to undercut the demand that she be treated as criminally responsible for her actions.

What allows these contradictions to enter this field of decisions is not simply the intrusion of paradoxical and disorganized social attitudes towards women. These may certainly exist, but the particular terms in which these contradictions appear in these texts actually derive from the structures of legal discourse itself. Their seeds are firmly planted in a feature of legal exculpations that was noted in the previous chapter. Within the established forms of legal argument the normality of a psychological response can be cited as grounds for either legal exculpation or the refusal of such exculpation – and so can the *abnormality* of a response. Criminal responsibility for an action can be undercut both on grounds that *no* normal person would behave like that (as in diminished responsibility), and on grounds that *any* normal person might do so (as in provocation). The paradoxes in the construction of women's legal responsibilitiy arise from an uneasy shifting between these two irreconcilable lines of reasoning. Female cases are constructed so that it is equally possible for them to come to rest on either side of that conceptual divide – with opposite effects in terms of the formal attribution of responsibility.

In practice, the vast majority of female defendants are held criminally responsible for at least some aspect of their behaviour. They are convicted of at least some crime, though maybe not the most serious one that might be inferred on the basis of their behaviour alone. And technically, this conviction closes these questions of their agency, responsibility and legal culpability, for it is only by formally constituting them as legally responsible actors that the court can legitimately pronounce them guilty. Once this initial decision has been reached, however, the court must then turn to the separate decision on the *sentencing* of the offender, and at this point all these questions are able to resurface, along with a host of others that up till now have been excluded. It is with the organization of this much wider field of judicial decision, where it is the sentence rather than the verdict that is at stake, that the remaining chapters will be concerned.

Notes

1 I have classed as 'homicides' all cases involving charges of murder, attempted murder, infanticide and manslaughter, irrespective of the final conviction. Brief details of all these cases are given in Table 2, Appendix B.

2 Chapter 2, note 7.

3 An average of six such statements were found in each male case, as compared to just under three in female cases – even though the female cases included twice as many lines of text overall, containing an average of three times as many statements relating to aspects of the offender's 'mental life'.

4 See Appendix B, Section 2iii.

5 In one instance only, in which the police were clearly unable to keep pace with the suspect's (spontaneously offered and very rambling) account of his motives, they are recorded as stopping him to ask if he has ever been in a mental hospital. When he says yes, they take down details of the dates and hospitals, and thereafter abandon the interview.

6 See Appendix B, Table 2: Cases 1, 4, 8, 9, 10, 11, 12, 13, 22.

7 Case 2.

8 Cases 80, 81, 84.

9 *Byrne, 1960, 3 All ER 1*. See also discussion of diminished responsibility, Chapter 2.

Chapter four:

Doctoring the sentence

The prisoner stands in the dock, found guilty of burgling a neighbour's house, stealing a radio and setting fire to some library books. Although he maintained his innocence throughout the trial, the finding of guilt has been straightforward. He never disputed any of the deeds charged against him: his plea of innocence was based only on the claim that the acts were justified. His neighbours, he maintained, had been using the radio to transmit obscene messages into his head and to render him sexually impotent. He had therefore decided to destroy the radio and had broken into the flat in order to get it. He had noticed the library books in the course of the burglary, and had realized that most of them were coded documents about himself. He had therefore put them all in the bath and set light to them, to show the neighbours that he knew what they were doing. Despite his unusual state of mind, there has never been any dispute that the man knew exactly what he was doing, and was aware that it was contrary to the law. There was thus no question of raising a defence of insanity, and as the judge made clear in his summing up to the jury, the defendant's own unchallenged evidence of his behaviour and intentions left no legal grounds for an acquittal.

It has taken just three hours for the court to find the man guilty. Convicted now, he gazes into space, and makes no response as the judge orders that he be detained in prison prior to sentence, pending the preparation of social and medical reports. A police officer shakes him gently and leads him back through a side door into some unpublic recess of the court. As he goes, there is a sudden disturbance in the public gallery. A young woman is standing up, solitary, ashen faced and shaking. 'Can't you see he's ill?', she shouts. '*You stupid fuckers can't you see he's ill?*' She is removed, protesting. The judge shakes his head gravely, and murmers to the empty gallery: 'Yes madam, we can see; we can see.' At this stage the judge is anxious to find some medical placement for the man. It will take five months, four custodial remands, two psychiatric reports and many medico-legal arguments before he finally abandons this hope, and reluctantly imposes a sentence of imprisonment.

As this case illustrates, a defendant's psychiatric condition, even if quite severe in clinical terms, can be irrelevant to the assessment of criminal responsibility. In the majority of cases mentally disordered offenders will be convicted or acquitted on precisely the same terms as mentally normal ones. Yet as the court moves from conviction to sentence, there is a radical change in the issues to be considered, and at this stage evidence of the offender's psychiatric condition can claim a renewed importance. In particular, the assertion of mental disorder can raise a whole series of dilemmas in relation to punishment. If the crime appears symptomatic of some medical disorder, then punishment may seem unjust or pointless. If the offender needs medical treatment, then any punishment that precludes it may seem inhumane. If medical treatment might prevent further offending, then a sentence that obstructs it may seem counter-productive. And if the offender is seriously disturbed or deranged, then normal forms of punishment may seem impractical or inconvenient. Over the past century, a series of medical and legal strategies have attempted to resolve these dilemmas, resulting in an accumulation of special provisions whereby convicted offenders can be subjected to psychiatric treatment, either instead of a penal sentence or in addition to it. The object of this chapter is to outline the background and structure of these various provisions, and to suggest some of the historical factors that underlie the sexual discrepancies in their current deployment. The more immediate determinants of this discrepancy will be examined in the following two chapters.

Servicing penality

The longest established of the various provisions for the psychiatric treatment of convicted offenders is that of the Prison Medical Service.[1] This service was established in the 1860s, as part of the major prison reforms that were taking place at the time,[2] and from its inception the treatment of the mentally deranged and abnormal was amongst the most pressing of its responsibilities. The situation has not changed: the treatment and containment of psychological problems is still the largest single component of the clinical work of prison doctors.[3]

The establishment of psychiatric facilities within the prisons was a response to two of the major dilemmas posed by the imprisonment of mentally abnormal offenders. In the first place, it allows the offender to be both treated *and* punished, thus evading the humanitarian objections to depriving a sick person of necessary medical care. In the second place, it reduces the logistical inconvenience of imprisoning the deranged. It ensures that where medically possible, the derangement will be cured or relieved, thus preventing it from interfering with the routine processes of punishment. And in cases of intractable derangement, it allows the aberrant prisoner to be medically segregated, thus transferring the problems of management to specialist personnel, and minimizing the disruption to the prison's normal discipline and morale.

The modesty of these objectives is related to the historical conditions out of which they arose. The reform of prisoners was at this point conceived in spiritual rather than medical or even psychological terms, and the natural ally of this project was therefore the priest rather than the doctor. The presence of medical disorders might be seen as disruptive to the work of reform, but it was not conceived as making offenders less guilty for their crimes, and no strong connection was drawn between the medical and the criminal failings of the prison population. The role accorded to doctors within this project was therefore essentially peripheral. Crime and disease were conceived as merely coincidental, and even if the professional status of the doctor allowed him to claim a particular respect within the prison hierarchy, his function was essentially peripheral to the reformatory project.

Since its introduction a century ago, the Prison Medical Service has been increasingly left behind by developments elsewhere in the medical field. It was never incorporated into the National Health Service, and has generally been reduced to the status of a poor relation of the Health Service, facing constant difficulties of recruitment, funding and facilities. And in relation to the treatment of mentally disordered offenders, its role has become particularly uncomfortable. The general agreement that the imprisonment of seriously disordered offenders is undesirable has meant that little priority has been given to the provision of psychiatric facilities in the prisons. What facilities there are, are disturbingly archaic.[4] Many of the doctors have no psychiatric qualifications, and except in the women's prisons there are generally no nurses at all. Meanwhile, the reality of sentencing practice means that these facilities are constantly stretched almost to breaking point. Very large numbers of disordered offenders are still consigned to prisons;[5] and despite all its shortcomings the Prison Medical Service is still required to do the bulk of the work of forensic psychiatry, and take responsibility for many of the most difficult of psychiatric cases. As I shall discuss in detail in the following chapters, many of the reasons for this situation can be traced to the limitations of the more modern provisions for psychiatric disposal. But in part it is also traceable to the persistence, amongst both sentencers and prison doctors themselves, of those same preoccupations and values that under-pinned the initial development of prison psychiatry.

On the judicial side, the continuing existence of the Prison Medical Service allows judges to assume that by imprisoning a disordered offender they are ensuring both the provision of psychiatric care and some form of penal sanction. And in cases where it is felt that the offender is wicked or dangerous 'as well' as disordered, this supposed combination of approaches may still be presented as particularly advantageous:

MAGISTRATE: 'Stand up Mr Nash. I have heard all about you from your solicitor and the police officer here. And as you know I have these reports from Dr

O'Connor and your probation officer. What you've been doing is a matter we take very seriously. Very seriously indeed. We can't let it go on. Do you understand?'

DEFENDANT: 'I'm not ... I wasn't ... [inaudible]

MAGISTRATE: 'Now I know you need help. This isn't the kind of thing a normal man engages in. And the doctor's report here says .... Hmmm [looks at report]. You are obviously a disturbed man, but I'm afraid this sort of thing is very disturbing to other people too. On count one I'm going to send you to prison for four months, and on count two, which is perhaps less worrying, I'm going to impose two months, to run concurrently. Four months altogether. The doctors there will be able to give you the kind of help you need, and I hope you'll take it. You have to get some help, but you also have to know what a dim view society takes on this sort of thing, and possibly this is help you can get in prison better than anywhere else. You were already seeing Dr O'Connor and I'm not sure you took this very seriously. I think in prison you'll be able to think about these things. Do you understand?'

(Transcript, Magistrate's Court, man convicted of indecent exposure)

Officially, this approach is now universally deplored, not only by the Home Office and leading authorities on sentencing, but also by the Prison Medical Service itself.[6] But there is also a sense in which Prison Medical officers are themselves implicated in maintaining and condoning this approach. For it is they who compile the majority of medical reports to the courts,[7] and the framework of expectations in which they still work, at least within the male prisons, is one which tends to militate *against* the psychiatric disposal of male offenders, even in cases where there may be clinical and legal grounds for such a course.

Where the sentencer requests pre-sentence psychiatric reports on a convicted offender, it is common practice, especially in male cases, to remand the case without bail, so that the offender will be detained in prison and the report will be prepared by the Prison Medical Service. The Prison Medical Service also contributes a large number of 'voluntary' psychiatric reports on prisoners remanded for other reasons. Through this work of forensic assessment, prison doctors exert a very major influence over the final selection of offenders for psychiatric disposal.

In a small proportion of cases, prison doctors are insistent in recommending a psychiatric disposal, or at least in advising that further specialist assessment is required before such a possibility should be discounted. These are generally cases involving either female offenders, or males whose behaviour is so gravely disturbed that their management in an ordinary prison environment is almost impossible. More typical, however, especially in cases involving males, is the striking *absence* of any such recommendations, even in cases involving quite serious disorder.

In my own sample, there were twenty two reports on male offenders in which prison medical officers diagnosed some form of psychiatric disorder. In only seven of these was there any recommendation either for treatment or for further psychiatric assessment. Other research suggests a similar pattern. Bowden, for example, in a study restricted to male cases,[8] found that prison doctors never made recommendations for psychiatric treatment on probation and in fact rarely made treatment recommendations at all. It was not that they perceived their charges as clinically *unsuitable* for psychiatric disposal. When questioned by researchers, these medical officers described a psychiatric disposal as the most desirable outcome for large numbers of the cases in the sample – even though in the majority of these cases they made no such recommendation to the court. They simply did not appear to regard it as part of their function to recommend treatment, except where the mental disorder would seriously interfere with a penal disposal. So far were their reports from *privileging* the medical needs of their patients that in most cases they seemed to find it impertinent even to *mention* those needs.

In the course of my interviews, several National Health Service doctors voiced frustration at the psychiatric reports produced by their colleagues in the Prison Service. From the perspective of hospital-based psychiatry, the central purpose of the psychiatric report is to provide authoritative advice on any need for psychiatric treatment, and to indicate whether a psychiatric disposal might be available or desirable. Against this background of expectations, the frequent failure of prison doctors to address these issues seemed at best bewildering and at worst quite reprehensible. As one doctor angrily remarked: 'I don't know how they can even *call* them psychiatric reports half the time. It's either an insult to the law or an insult to psychiatry, I'm not sure which.'

What makes these omissions intelligible, however, and also underpins the apparent complicity of the Prison Medical Service with the continuing imprisonment of disordered offenders, is the position from which the writers of these reports are addressing the court. They adopt that same modest and peripheral position that was established for the prison doctors over a century ago. They speak as loyal employees of the prisons, whose task is to provide a specific professional service, and whose responsibilities are largely confined to the detection and treatment of subjects whose medical condition might pose management problems for his employers. Above all, these documents confirm the proper discharge of official duties: they indicate any disorder that has been detected and they document any medical actions that have been taken. Accordingly, there is little attempt to disguise the institutional interests that underlie the organization of the report. If the disorder seems likely to prove seriously disruptive to the prison, these reports will sometimes recommend an external referral or a medical disposal. If the disorder is troublesome only to the offender, they generally indicate that any necessary treatment can either be given in prison or else can be deferred until the prisoner is at liberty.[9] They rarely presume to address the court on matters outside this limited frame; the nearest they generally come to a recommendation is the implicitly damning conclusion: 'This offender is fit for any penalty that the court may impose'.[10]

I have deliberately referred to *male* offenders here, since this is an approach which is almost entirely confined to the medical officers in male prisons. Although the female prisons are also served by the Prison Medical Service, there is actually little to distinguish the reports on women that are prepared inside and outside the prison. To understand this, it is necessary to look at the differences between women's prisons and men's, for as I shall discuss in a moment, the place that medical personnel have historically secured for themselves in the women's prisons is conceptually rather special.

From competition to collaboration

Like its original forbear of a century ago, the Prison Medical Service of the present day is generally a rather constrained and subservient creature. Yet the modesty of its current status represents a reversal of its fortunes. For there was a brief epoch in its history when even an equal partnership with the penal authorities would not have satisfied its ambitions: for a brief moment psychiatry actually sought to *supplant* penality. Ultimately this strategy failed, but as with other developments in the field, its localized achievements were never completely superseded or dismantled, but have left their legacy in the general medley of available options and provisions. This legacy is particularly important both in the women's prisons and in the provisions for psychiatric treatment on probation.

To eradicate crime by curing ... a hospital not a prison

Medicine entered the prisons at the point when their reformatory project was first being established, but it was not until the initially 'spiritual' conception of this project gave way to a more secular and 'scientific' one that medicine achieved any privileged influence there. A central impetus in its development was the emergence and popularization of psychoanalysis, in the 1920s. The psychoanalytic approach that was being developed in Britain at this point[11] was an almost unequivocally normative one, which cheerfully defined all criminal, delinquent and antisocial behaviour as a sign of inner maladjustment. It thus provided a basis for the extension of forensic psychiatry from a limited group of conspicuously deranged offenders to the whole criminal population. It was a fashionable approach, and several of the influential prison doctors of this period became enthusiastic converts.

Once accepted, its political implications were inescapable: before long, there were calls for a radical reconstruction of the whole philosophy of penal treatment. For example, a 1932 report commissioned by the Medical Research Council contains a detailed and concrete proposal for the total medicalization of the penal system. Whilst acknowledging that 'it would not be reasonable to suggest that such a system could replace the penal system all at once', the author, (herself a prison doctor), goes on to propose that:

It is possible ... that the plans suggested could be started as an experiment and
the details of its working must be in accordance with the premise that crime is a
symptom of underlying defect or disease .... Although this is a system to deal
with crime, the buildings should be called hospitals and not prisons, since the
object will be to eradicate crime by curing, through psychological treatment
and other measures, the underlying psychological maladjustments and defects;
whereas in the case of prisons the object is the eradication of crime by means of
punishment.

(Pailthorpe, 1932(1) p. 97f)

The experimental establishment of such an institution received official
approval, and despite several decades of practical setbacks and delays which
prevented the actual building of such an institution,[12] the psychiatric
approach to criminality gained an increasing acceptance as the politically
progressive model for penal reform. In almost every aspect of penal
treatment, psychiatrists gained increasing power, and for several decades the
possibility of a new medical hegemony seemed only just over the penal
horizon.

As things turned out, however, the promise never materialized.
Somewhere during the 1950s and 1960s, the tide turned, and the brief
momentum of this psychiatric strategy was suddenly exhausted. The
reported crime rate was rapidly rising; the prisons were again becoming
overcrowded. On the one hand this meant that the urgent concern for prison
psychiatrists – no less than other prison personnel – again shifted from
reforming the prisoners to simply controlling and containing them. And on
the other hand, it allowed the therapeutic approach to become something of a
scapegoat for the manifest failures of the penal system. A new wave of
conservative criticism decried the 'soft' conditions in prisons and in place of a
rehabilitative approach, called for the reinstatment of deterrence,
denouncement and retribution.[13] In this sterner climate, the grand
therapeutic design that would have turned prisons into hospitals now seemed
embarrassingly fanciful rather than progressive. There was no denouement,
no dramatic reversal of policy. By a series of small cuts the brief privilege of
psychiatry within the prisons was quietly undermined, until the following
decade it gradually returned, to all intents and purposes, to its former
subservient status.

Significantly, the only exception to this was in the women's prisons. In
1968 the Secretary of State announced plans for the rebuilding of Holloway as
a new, therapeutically orientated prison, to be the main custodial facility for
women in England and Wales:

Following a review of the custodial arrangements for women and girls, I have
decided upon a programme to reshape the system of female penal
establishments in England and Wales ....

Most women and girls in custody require some form of medical, psychiatric
or remedial treatment. The main feature of the programme is ... the building of
an establishment that is basically a secure hospital to act as the hub of the

female penal system. Its medical and psychiatric facilities will be its central feature, and normal custodial facilities will comprise a relatively small part of the establishment.

(Callaghan, Hansard, 16.12.68)

This new Holloway was the only general prison whose concept, design and management ever approached the thoroughgoing medical model proposed by the psychiatric reformers of the 1930s. This model, which was rapidly being eased aside in the male prisons, was still conceived as entirely worthy, acceptable and progressive for women offenders. It was not only a selected, atypical and specifically disordered minority of female prisoners who were seen as appropriate subjects for the medical approach. It was the whole population of the prison. Most of them, it is stated, 'require' medical treatment – and by implication, the remainder may at least be *treated* as if they required it.[14] The new Holloway was completed in the early 1970s, and stands, bricks and warders alike, a monument to the medical model of penal rehabilitation.

The privilege that the women's prisons have accorded to psychiatry is also evident in the reports and recommendations of their resident doctors. Unlike the closely circumscribed reports from male prisons, the medical reports on women prisoners are complex documents, containing statements on a whole range of biographical, social, moral, criminal, psychological aspects of their subjects' lives, as well as a detailed discussion of their mental condition. Expectations of extensive medical authority and expertise are also reflected in the conclusions of these reports. Whether or not any mental disorder is diagnosed, medical officers from the women's prisons quite routinely include detailed reflections on the ideal sentencing and management of the offenders concerned. In these reports one rarely finds the dismissive formula that concludes so many male reports: 'I can find no evidence of mental disorder *and have therefore no recommendation to make.*'

It is also significant, however, that these recommendations are rarely in favour of the imprisonment of disordered female offenders. In the decades since the new Holloway was opened, progressive psychiatry has moved steadily away from institutional provision, and towards a new model of 'community care', in which all institutional treatment is viewed with suspicion, and enclosed, custodial facilities are particularly disfavoured. The medical officers of Holloway are sensitive to these new trends. They are also keenly aware of the widespread public criticism of the prison's own psychiatric provisions, repeatedly documenting their failures even to protect their inmates from harm, let alone provide a suitable milieu for therapy. The admission of yet more disordered offenders to Holloway not only runs counter to the newer philosophies of modern psychiatry, but also compounds the institution's existing crisis of credibility. The privileged emphasis on psychiatry which characterizes the women's prisons thus assumes an ironic aspect. Rather than drawing disordered offenders *into* the women's prisons, the additional authority which this emphasis accords to the psychiatrist is as far as possible deployed to keep such offenders *out*.

Probation and the mental condition of offenders

Another offshoot from the psychotherapeutic approach towards crime was the development of the psychiatric probation order. There had in any case been something of a tradition of placing mentally disordered offenders on probation. The Probation of Offenders Act of 1907, which first established a formal Probation Service, had explicitly mentioned the 'mental condition of the offender' among the possible grounds for choosing such a disposal. In 1907, however, there were no public psychiatric facilities outside the asylums, and thus little opportunity for probationers to receive any actual psychiatric treatment. In the early 1920s however, a series of psychoanalytically orientated out-patient clinics were opened,[15] and the emergent probation service was quick to establish both practical and conceptual links with them.

Prior to psychoanalysis, probationary supervision was something of a well-meaning practice waiting for a theory. Progressive and compatible, the arrival of psychoanalysis promised precisely such a theory. The principle of 'transference' offered scientific credentials for the importance of the probationary 'relationship'; the principle of uncovering unconscious motivation provided a basis for its reformatory 'work'; and the principle of resistance explained its failures. Furthermore, the practical arrangements through which psychoanalysis was conducted were in many ways directly analogous to those under which, (willy nilly), the probation service was required to 'supervise' its subjects. From the perspective of the more established 'disciplinary' model of correction, the discontinuity, remoteness and lack of material surveillance that are intrinsic to probation could only appear as serious shortcomings. The model of psychoanalysis, on the other hand, at the very heart of which was the singular, formal, ritualized and circumscribed relationship of the therapeutic 'session', allowed a methodological virtue to be made of this organizational necessity.

The probation service was thus quick to seize on the psychodynamic approach, which even now remains a significant feature of its practice.[16] (It is striking, for example, that the social enquiry reports produced by probation officers are often far more attentive to the psychological aspects of their cases than are the corresponding reports produced by psychiatrists.) In the 1920s and 1930s the psychoanalytically orientated clinics, particularly the Tavistock, became virtually the training centres for the developing probation service,[17] which in turn provided these clinics with many of their patients. This alliance was recognized by the courts and resulted in an increasingly widespread practice of placing mentally disordered offenders on probation, with the understanding that the probation officer would arrange for psychiatric referral. The 1948 Criminal Justice Act finally formalized this practice by allowing the courts to make psychiatric treatment an explicit condition of a probation order, thereby establishing the first of the formal psychiatric disposals for convicted offenders.

The current provisions for psychiatric probation orders are set out in the 1973 Powers of the Criminal Courts Act, which reproduces the original 1948 provisions almost verbatim:

> 3. (1) Where the court is satisfied, on the evidence of a duly qualified medical practitioner ... that the mental condition of the offender is such as requires and may be susceptible to treatment, but is not such as to warrant his detention in pursuance of a Hospital Order under Part V [of the Mental Health Act 1959], the court may, if it makes a probation order, include the requirement that the offender shall submit during the whole of the probation period or during such part of the period as may be specified in that order, to treatment by or under the direction of a duly qualified medical practitioner with a view to the improvement of the offender's mental condition.
>
> (2) The treatment required by any such order shall be such of one of the following kinds of treatment as may be specified in the order, that is to say:
>
> (a) treatment as a resident patient in a hospital or mental nursing home ...
> (b) treatment as a non resident patient in such an institution or place as may be specified in the order or
> (c) treatment by or under the direction of such duly qualified medical practioner as may be specified in the order.
>
> (Powers of the Criminal Courts Act, 1973, s 3)

Over the years since these provisions were first established, the psychoanalytic approach has generally become less influential, and it is now extremely rare for offenders dealt with under these provisions to be referred for analytic psychotherapy; much more commonly, they will be treated by general psychiatrists in ordinary psychiatric wards or out-patient clinics, and will receive an eclectic mixture of drugs and informal therapeutic 'support'. None the less, the historical origin of these provisions has left a significant legacy for the ways in which this form of disposal can now be used.

First, its criteria for offering treatment reflect a very broad conception of psychiatry's contribution to the treatment of deviance. The legislations does not defer to the 'disease' model of psychiatric involvement, and actually does not require that the offender be psychiatrically disordered. All that it demands is that the 'mental condition' of the offender is such that he or she 'requires and may be susceptible to treatment' – a formulation that was deliberately broad enough to encompass any case where an analytically oriented therapist might be willing to become involved, including many where no doctor would call the offender 'ill'.

Second, the wording of the Act reflects the diversity of settings and personnel involved in psychoanalytic treatment at that time – including therapists with and without medical qualifications, working in hospital, clinics, and private practice. The Act places no restriction on the setting and content of any medical treatment and allows treatment to be carried out by non-medical personnel working only 'under the direction' of a qualified doctor. In practice this means that the subject of these provisions need not take up a hospital bed unless the doctor so wishes, and may in fact receive only the most nominal of psychiatric supervision, such as an occasional home visit or out-patient appointment. Alternatively, the psychiatrist responsible for the disposal may delegate the whole burden of treatment to some non-medical colleague, such as a community nurse, clinical psychologist, or non-medical therapist. Indeed, it appears that a large proportion of offenders dealt with by these orders never see a psychiatrist at all.[18]

Finally, the terms of the provisions reflect the expectation of an ongoing working partnership between psychiatric and judicial agents. The offender receiving treatment is still under a probation order, and if he or she either refuses to cooperate with medical treatment, or else remains troublesome despite it, he or she may be returned to the court, in which case a penal sentence may be substituted for probation. This means that doctors are not obliged to take total responsibility for the offender, and have a let-out clause available if the medical approach goes drastically wrong.

Against this background, it is easy to understand the attractiveness of this form of disposal to the doctors involved. The terms of the provisions serve to maximize the medical discretion and minimize the medical burden. It is curious that these orders receive such scant attention in the medical and penal literature, and are often treated as only a rather minor aspect of psychiatric involvement with offenders: in fact they are easily the commonest form of psychiatric disposal. They are also the form of disposal where the sexual disparity is the greatest. As will become clear in Chapter 6, the conceptual and legislative framework of such orders, (which primarily facilitate the out-patient treatment of cooperative petty offenders suffering minor or nondescript disorders), is one which fits rather ill with the general expectations of psychiatric involvement with male offenders, but is neatly tailored to the characteristics, needs, abilities and deserts that both the courts and forensic psychiatrists typically attribute to women.

The Mental Health Act: compromise and consensus

The most recent legislation providing for the treatment of mentally abnormal offenders appears in the Mental Health Acts of 1959 and 1983.[19] Although in other areas of mental health provision the 1983 Act makes significant departures from the previous Act of 1959, the sections dealing with offenders remain substantially unchanged.

Under the provisions of this Act, the courts can order the admission of a mentally disordered offender to hospital, as an alternative to a penal sentence.[20] Admission will normally be to a National Health Service psychiatric hospital, a psychiatric unit in a local General Hospital, or to one of the Special Hospitals, (Broadmoor, Rampton, Moss Side and Park Lane), which offer psychiatric treatment under conditions of secure detention. Once admitted, the offender is in a similar position to any other compulsorily detained psychiatric patient, and all responsibility for his or her treatment, including the decision as to discharge, passes to the relevant medical consultant: the criminal justice system normally has no further rights over the case. In cases where there may be risk to the public, however, a Crown Court can, at the point when the order is made, impose a Restriction Order, which prohibits the hospital from discharging the offender unless his or her release has first been authorized by the Secretary of State.

The criteria and conditions which must be satisfied before a hospital order can be made are set out in Section 37 of the 1983 Act:[21]

(1) [that the] person is convicted before the Crown Court of an offence punishable with imprisonment other than an offence the sentence for which is fixed by law, or is convicted by a Magistrates' Court of an offence punishable on summary conviction with imprisonment and ....

(2) ... (a) the court is satisfied, on the written or oral evidence of two registered medical practitioners that the offender is suffering from mental illness, psychopathic disorder, severe mental impairment or mental impairment and that either –

  (i) the mental disorder from which the offender is suffering is of a nature and degree which makes it appropriate for him to be detained in hospital for medical treatment and, in the case of psychopathic disorder or mental impairment, that such treatment is likely to alleviate or prevent a deterioration of his condition: or

  (ii) in the case of an offender who has attained the age of 16 years the mental disorder is of a nature or degree which warrants his reception into guardianship under this Act; and

(b) the court is of the opinion, having regard to all the circumstances including the nature of the offence and the character and antecedents of the offender and to other available methods of dealing with him, that the most suitable method of disposing of the case is by means of an order under this section [and] ....

(4) ... the court is satisfied on the written or oral evidence of the registered medical practitioner who would be in charge of his treatment or of some other person representing the managers of the hospital that arrangements have been made for his admission to that hospital.

(Mental Health Act, 1983, s 37)

These modern provisions reflect a rather different relationship between psychiatry and criminal justice from that of either of the earlier strategies of psychiatric provision for offenders. The arrangements for treatment in prison made psychiatry little more than a servant of criminal justice, and treated the provision of psychiatric care as generally peripheral to the objectives of judicial sentencing. And the arrangements for treatment on probation tended to make partners of psychiatry and criminal justice, and implied their close collaboration in a shared project of readjustment and rehabilitation. In contrast to both of these, the new provisions assume a relationship in which psychiatry and criminal justice stand opposite each other as distinct alternatives. The imposition of a hospital order precludes any penal sentence, and once a hospital order has been passed, the offender becomes the responsibility of the psychiatric system, and cannot then be returned to the court except in the context of some completely new offence. All negotiation between psychiatry and criminal justice over the proper disposal of the offender must thus take place prior to the moment of sentencing. Accordingly, the medical and judicial criteria that must be met before such an order is made are particularly complex and detailed.

First there are 'qualifying conditions', which must be fulfilled before a hospital order can even be considered. On the criminological side, the law requires that the offender must be one on whom a prison sentence could be imposed, but for whom the penalty is not fixed by law, (the latter being, effectively, a reference to murder). These conditions seem aimed at ensuring a rough equity between mentally disordered and mentally normal offenders, by restricting the medical detention of disordered offenders to cases where mentally sound ones could also be deprived of their liberty, and at the same time preventing disordered offenders from gaining special treatment in cases where mentally sound ones could claim no mitigation of their sentence. On the medical side, the law requires that the offender must be diagnosed as suffering from one of the four varieties of formal mental disorder that are specified in the Act: mental illness, mental impairment, severe mental impairment or psychopathic disorder. This restriction seems aimed at producing a similar rough equity between criminal and non-criminal patients. It restricts the hospital orders for offenders to cases where non-offenders might also qualify for compulsory hospitalization under civil provisions of the Act.

On the face of it, neither of these criteria seem particularly favourable to the psychiatrization of women. The criterion of imprisonability effectively favours *men*, since it is they who are more commonly convicted of the more serious (imprisonable) offences. And the restriction of these orders to the more serious categories of disorder should also tip the balance in favour of men. Although there is a conspicuous excess of females in the general psychiatric population, males do account for a large proportion of those diagnosed under those relatively severe categories of disorder that meet the Mental Health Act requirements. It is only in the classification of mental illness that one finds a marked excess of female cases; even here, the female excess is concentrated in the more mild and minor forms of illness, which might be deemed insufficient to qualify, whilst in the severest forms of psychotic illness, which most unambiguously satisfy the Mental Health Act criteria, there is actually an excess of *male* cases.[22] In principle, both of these initial criminal and clinical qualifications should thus tend to counteract rather than exaggerate any tendency towards a female excess in the use of these provisions. In practice, however, as I shall discuss in the next two chapters, things do not work out quite as one might expect.

If these initial medical and criminological qualifications are satisfied, the decision to impose or withhold a hospital order then focuses on two parallel questions. The first, posed to the examining doctor, is whether it is 'appropriate' to detain the offender in hospital. The second, posed to the sentencer, is whether this medical detention is 'the most suitable method of disposal'. Both questions must be answered affirmatively before a hospital order can be imposed, and thus either medical or judicial personnel can block the imposition of a hospital order.

It is clear both from the formulation of the law itself and from the conventions and precedents that have formed around it, that these issues of 'suitability' and 'appropriateness' may be assessed by reference to a wide assortment of institutional, juridical and practical considerations. They imply no particular philosophical perspective, but are immensely elastic concepts, capable of conforming themselves to whatever values seem most conveniently to hand: utility, justice, compassion, public safety, individual wellbeing, medical expedience or whatever. And as Chapter 6 will demonstrate, rather different criteria seem to come to hand in male and female cases.

Finally, the Act imposes a question about the availability of options. On the judicial side, the court is required to consider the 'other available methods of dealing with' the offender before determining that hospitalization is the 'most suitable method of disposing of the case'. And on the medical side, the law requires an assurance that if a hospital order is to be made, then a medical placement will in fact be made available. The Act establishes no terms on which a hospital or doctor can be *constrained* to take charge of any offender, and in practice doctors are thus free to veto the imposition of any hospital order simply by stating that appropriate facilities are not available. The important point is that the Health Service is free to make as much or as little provision as it pleases for the treatment of disordered offenders – and apart from a few tokenistic gestures, it has generally chosen to do very little in this area.

Here as elsewhere, the involvement of psychiatry in the treatment of offenders has been critically influenced by much wider trends in the development of psychiatry. Over the past few decades, mental health policy has favoured a move (of both patients and resources) away from custodial care and into 'the community'. The secure and long-term facilities that many forensic patients are deemed to need are an unfashionable rarity in modern psychiatric units, and even where central funds have been allocated for the provision of secure custodial units, the local Health Authorities have dragged their heels in establishing them.[23] At the same time, the political trend within psychiatry had been away from coercive treatment, and the association of psychiatric technologies with penal control has become a matter of embarrassment and unease within the medical establishment. Accordingly, the courts have found it increasingly difficult in recent years to make hospital orders for disordered offenders, even where they clearly regard hospitalization as the *only* suitable disposal.[24] Like so many other factors, the question of institutional availability impacts unequally on the disposal of male and female offenders, and again, as I shall discuss in the following chapters, it is the hospitalization of male offenders that has been particularly threatened by these most recent developments of psychiatric provision.

The various threads that I have traced through this chapter do not weave together into any single regular cloth. Over the past century, successive generations of doctors, administrators, legislators and sentencers have constituted a variety of offenders as posing medico-penal 'problems', and have attempted to resolve these problems in various extemporary ways, in accordance with the favoured philosophies of their time. Development has been unsystematic, and its net result is a field of psychiatric involvement with offenders that is internally inconsistent and sometimes disorganized and contradictory. Institutionally, psychiatric services for offenders are dispersed between the National Health Service, the Prison Medical Service, the special hospitals, private medicine and the social services.[25] Legally, the provision of these services is governed by an assortment of unrelated statutes, which impose different criteria of involvement, and are predicated on different models of psychiatric activity. Clinically, the accumulation of alternative psychiatric strategies has allowed psychiatrists to offer treatment to offenders who are *not* classified as mentally disordered, but has by no means obliged them to offer treatment to offenders who *are*.

The very diversity of available options, (and of rationales for using them), introduces an immense flexibility into the decision-making process, and this of itself provides the basic conditions of discretion within which arbitrary biases – including sexual ones – can easily be activiated. Furthermore, an analysis of the criteria that are invoked in relation to these various options reveals that in many cases they related to issues that are already, prior to their activation in this context, commonly construed differently in male and female subjects. The following two chapters will illustrate and analyse these differences.

Notes

1 See Walker and McCabe (1973, Chapters 1–3) for a brief and valuable history of these developments.
2 Foucault (1977) gives a detailed analysis of the major changes in the practices and philosophies of penality that led to the 'reformatory prisons' of the Victorian era.
3 More than 40 per cent of the prescription-only medicines administered to prisoners are tranquillizers, anti-depressants, hypnotics, sedatives, and drugs used to control the side effects of major tranquillizers (*Annual Report of the Prison Medical Service*, 1984).
4 See Carlen (1986) for a balanced account of the psychiatric work of the prison medical service. See also Cohen and Taylor (1976) for a discussion of the secrecy that surrounds this work.
5 This point is discussed at greater length in Chapter 7. See Coid (1984) for a discussion of statistics relating to the mental health of the prison population.

6 See comments of the Butler Committee, reproduced as authority in the Home Office sentencing manual, *The Sentence of the Court*: 'It is undesirable to convey to the offender the impression that medical treatment will certainly be given to him in prison .... If, as frequently happens, it turns out that he does not receive medical treatment ... the offender may feel that he has a grievance against the authorities'. For the response of the prisons, see Butler (1975, para 11.5); Orr (1978).

7 No figures are published relating the total number of psychiatric reports received by the courts, although the Prison Statistics include details of reports compiled in prison. Both my own and previous studies (e.g. Gibbens *et al.* 1977) suggest that well over half of all male reports and approaching a half of all female reports are prepared in prison.

8 Bowden (1978).

9 e.g. male cases 80, 95, 101, 106, 108, 113, 123, 124.

10 Medical etiquette forbids doctors actually to *recommend* penal sanctions, although the force of this circumlocution is clear. This or similar comment concludes prison medical reports in cases 62, 65, 75, 77, 98, 101, 104, 106, 107, 109, 110, 115, 122 in all of which the medical officers had disgnosed some disorder.

11 e.g. Dove-Wilson (1932); East and Hubert (1939); Pailthorpe (1932 (1 & 2)).

12 What was eventually built was Grendon Prison, a much more modest institution than originally planned, which caters to the special needs of a highly selected group of mentally abnormal offenders. See Gunn *et al.* (1978) for an account of its work.

13 See for example, Devlin, 1963; Harris, 1979. For the change of emphasis, compare the descriptions of the functions of prison psychiatry in the Home Office publication of 1959 and 1969. See also Walker and McCabe (1973, p. 47f).

14 Thus, for example, women's prisons employ large numbers of qualified psychiatric nurses, who are not trained as discipline staff but still have general responsibilities in the management of 'normal' inmates. (In the male prisons, by contrast, even the *hospital* wings do not have trained nurses).

15 Such as the Portman Clinic and the Tavistock Square Clinic, both of which still operate today.

16 This approach clearly survives in practice, despite the recent emergence of an alternative 'non-treatment' model of probation work, as described in Bottoms and McWilliams (1979); Haxby (1978).

17 See Rose (1985, Chapter 8).

18 Forensic psychiatrists whom I interviewed in 1983 suggested that many offenders on out-patient psychiatric probation orders would only be seen once or twice. Lewis (1980, p. 11f) and Gibbens *et al.* (1981, p. 328f) suggest that up to a fifth of offenders on psychiatric probation orders will never see a psychiatrist at all.

19 Many of the cases in this study were adjudicated before the 1983 legislation came into force, but no differences were found in the discussion and decision-making relating to cases before and after the 1983 Act. See Appendix B.

20 Mental Health Act 1983, s 37.

21 Section 60 of the 1959 Mental Health Act makes almost identical provisions.

22 DHSS Statistics on Mental Health, 1984.

23 See Higgins (1984) in Craft and Craft, (eds), (1984).

24 In certain cases, where hospitalization of mentally disordered offenders has been blocked by non-medical hospital staff, judges have gone so far as to threaten

'contempt of court' proceedings against the agents involved. See for example Law Report in *The Times*, 15.6.83. Where it is doctors who are refusing admission, however, the courts do not have even this limited power, but must accept the medical opinion.

25 The modern trend is towards increasing social work and Social Services involvement in the care and management of mentally disordered offenders. The reduction in hospital facilities for the mentally disordered will doubtless further this process.

Chapter five:

Playing the labels

'Well first they need a ticket to the psychiatrist – that's pretty much a lottery for a start-off, unless they go private. We can't send *everyone*. And what comes back is anyone's guess. Toss a dice! Score a six, and it's schizophrenia so they go to hospital; anything else and they generally don't. Call it depression and they'll probably end up with *us*. It's all the same offender. It's a name-game. It's just playing the labels.'

(Probation officer)

The selection of particular offenders as in need of psychiatric treatment is generally a two-stage process. Initially, one or more of the ordinary agents of criminal justice will identify the case as one in which a psychiatric referral might be appropriate. The subject will then be referred to a psychiatrist, who will assess his or her condition and forward a written report to the court. About 5 per cent of criminal offenders are examined by a psychiatrist at some point during their trial. The two stages of assessment are governed by quite different preoccupations, and the lay and medical authorities often come to quite different conclusions. It is therefore appropriate to deal with the two stages of assessment separately.

The ground level of madness

'We see a lot of it in our work. We get a feel for it, we have to. Especially out on the beat, 'ground level', so to speak. What makes me laugh is when we've picked up a complete *nutter* (and half the time it's only because that's the only way to make sure a doctor sees them) and then the doctor comes back saying there's nothing the matter. Nothing the matter! Actually, it doesn't make us laugh. It makes us *livid*.'

(Police officer)

None of the criminal justice agents to whom I spoke suggested that they had any difficulty in detecting the cases needing psychiatric attention. Sometimes this entailed only the reactivation of a prior diagnosis. Many disordered offenders 'do the rounds', and become familiar figures whose histories of psychiatric involvement are well known to the local police, probation officers and magistrates. But in addition, members of each of the professional groups also engage in their own independent assessment of the offenders with whom they deal, whether or not any past psychiatric history is known. As one police officer insisted:

> 'The whole system would break down if we didn't have a nose for it ourselves: we can't know all of them, and we can't rely on a mental case telling us "Oh yes, and by the way I'm a mental case" …. It's part of our skills, see: we're the one that talks to them, and we have to get a feel for it.'

The professional training of each of the groups includes at least a token attention to aspects of psychiatric disorder, mental health law and psychiatry, but these officials frequently stressed to me that their real understanding of this field was something that they had to learn 'on the job'. Frequently these agents regarded themselves as lay experts in psychiatry. A typical comment would begin by conceding 'Of course I'm not a psychiatrist', but then go on to insist, 'I can always tell a psychiatric case when I see one!'

These non-medical agents shared a loosely similar perspective in these preliminary identifications, and offered me a more or less consistent picture of the kind of cases that they would refer for psychiatric attention. Their 'typical mental case' involved an offender who has committed an 'abnormal' or 'shocking' or 'pointless' offence; who responds bizarrely to the initial interventions of criminal justice personnel, (perhaps by being unrealistically resistent to the criminal justice process, or inappropriately unconcerned about it); who indulges in incomprehensible or outrageous behaviour, (such as publicly undressing in court); who inexplicably laughs, shouts or weeps; or who, (above all), says things that are unintelligible, out of place, preposterously improbable, or incoherent. This stage lunatic of the criminal justice system is also, insistently, *male*:

> 'I'll tell you the kind of case. This man was sitting in the dock laughing to himself; well, he was hallucinating. A West Indian – but he'd been in custody for a week so he wasn't on drugs or anything. Then he tried to climb out and had to be restrained two or three times. Not violent, just not all there. Then he wouldn't answer the charge, didn't know what was going on or *anything*. We put it to him several times, but it was getting farcical. And eventually I remanded the case because we couldn't, obviously, go on with it …. One thinks "Well if *that's* not a mental case, then what is?"'
>
> (Stipendiary magistrate)

When I commented to my interviewees on the invariable maleness of their depictions of the 'typical disordered offender', I was quickly informed that there were actually very few disordered females 'in the system'. Several respondents went so far as to say that they had *never* seen a female defendant who was 'really mad'. In absolute terms, of course, this rarity of disordered females entirely corresponds to the statistical figures. Female offenders are a small proportion of all offenders, and even though they are proportionally more likely than male offenders to be treated psychiatrically, the numbers involved are still tiny. This absolute disproportion in the number of male and female cases is not the whole of the story, however. There are also more complex differences in the terms in which the mental state of male and female offenders appeared to be *interpreted* by the personnel involved.

While insisting that they rarely if ever met female offenders who were 'really mad', these professional agents nevertheless gave descriptions of women who *behaved* in quite the same ways as their stereotypical madmen. In these female cases, however, such behaviour was not automatically interpreted as evidence of mental disorder:

> 'Of course we do *get* females going on like that: quite often really, they throw hysterics, cry, scream, get that sort of thing. They can get really *nasty* some of them' [laughs] … 'scratch you, pull your hair, that sort of thing. Either that or just break down. But with women it's more normal hysterics. No offence, but women *are* more emotional, I think. And some young lads in the force don't known how to handle them. With women you have to play it by ear. We don't get many real nutters among the women, not what you'd call really mental, but we do get a fair bit of trouble from some of them.'
>
> (Police officer)

A related notion was expressed by a magistrate. She had been describing in detail a 'mental' case where the defendant had been a 'quivering mute' throughout his trial, and 'broke down in tears, floods of tears' when asked if he had anything he wished to say to the court. She then added, as an afterthought:

> 'If it's a man, you take it seriously, something like that. I don't mean men shouldn't ever cry, of course they should. […] But if a man does cry in court, I do think there might be something to take quite seriously there. It's much more normal with a woman. A woman in the dock she'll quite often cry at the end or often in cross examination. Or get tongue-tied. It's just much more *normal* in a woman. I don't think that means she's mentally ill; I think we just have to be that much more sensitive with a woman, especially a first offender. The court can be a very frightening place.'
>
> (Lay magistrate)

In declining to pathologize this emotional behaviour in women, criminal justice personnel are making allowances for its feminine 'normality'. And equally 'normal', according to several of my respondents, was a certain deviousness of women, that might lead them to pretend madness in order to gain certain advantages. As one probation officer remarked:

> 'Word's got round about the shoplifting lark: some of them think they've just got to say they were depressed. "Having a period" – that's another favourite. Or they act crazy in court, or when you interview them they go deliberately doolally [....] All a try on. You do need a lot of experience.'
>
> (Probation officer)

Given this seeming reluctance to construe female offenders as 'mad', even in circumstances where a male offender would routinely be defined thus, it may seem odd that so many female offenders are still referred to psychiatrists for reports. The keys to this lie first in a different conception of 'mental troubles' in female offenders, and second in the different function that the referral of female offenders is typically expected to fulfil. Both of these factors are related to issues already discussed in relation to the assessment of criminal responsibility.

As described in Chapter 3, male offenders are typically conceived as 'external' creatures, inhabiting a public and observable world of events and behaviours. Correspondingly, what appears as 'disorder' in a male offender is typically a visible and public derangement at the level of observable behaviour, that psychiatry may be called upon to control or contain. The subjectivity of women, by contrast, is typically conceived in terms of inner events and feelings, whose relationship to the external is inherently ambiguous and problematic. Accordingly, the mental disorders of female offenders are typically conceptualized as rather private and internal troubles, that psychiatry might make accessible, understandable and manipulable. These 'troubles' come in two basic forms: one, the traumas of emotions and inner experiences, characterized by states of depression and anxiety, and two, the troubles that arise in the problematic 'mediation' of women's relationships with others, problems of communication, and problems of personality. Admittedly, these troubles of female existence are not construed as 'real madness', and so the troubled female offender is not regularly characterized as a 'typical mental case'. But they are still troubles in which psychiatrists are assumed to possess a special expertise, and female offenders who appear to be thus afflicted make up a large proportion of the offenders remanded for psychiatric assessment.

These internal troubles define a domain of loosely 'neurotic' pathology which in male cases appears to be generally ignored or discounted. It is not that male offenders actually fail to exhibit the range of signs and symptoms that are interpreted in this way in relation to women. Reticence, misery, social isolation and disturbance of domestic relationships: reading the reports of probation officers or the police, it would seem that in fact these are troubles that characterize male and female offenders equally. In male cases, however, such signs are rarely read as anything except the common surliness or antisocial personality of the 'ordinary criminal': it is only in female cases that they are regularly given any significance as evidence of mental pathology.

Unlike the florid madness of the 'typical mental case', which criminal justice personnel feel quite competent to recognize and identify, these internal, neurotic, and generally female troubles occupy an ambiguous place within the criminological conception of disorder. In the first place, their pathological status is treated as less clearcut and self-evident than that of the 'typical mental case'. Accordingly, the medical referral in such cases is not necessarily directed, (as so often in male cases), towards the punctual transfer of an 'obviously mad' offender from judicial to medical control; instead it often represents a quite open-ended and genuine request for diagnostic advice and clarification.

Second, and irrespective of the diagnosis, there is only a hazy boundary between these factors of nominally 'psychiatric' distress and all the other mitigations that may excite the sympathy and pity of the court. The predominantly female cases that are referred to psychiatrists under this rubric of 'mental problems' are often cases in which, (as so often in female cases), the offender has been presented as a *generally* harmless or pathetic or tragic individual, and it is this rather unspecific mitigation that has made the sentencing a matter of anxiety to the court. Confronted, for example, with an offender who has been simultaneously convicted of a serious crime and presented as the 'victim of a tragedy', the court may simply not know what to do.

In such cases, any possibility of psychiatric treatment, (with or without any formal diagnosis of disorder), will often be enthusiastically pursued, as a means of avoiding a penal sentence. Even in the absence of any serious hope of treatment, the securing of psychiatric advice in such cases may serve the important rhetorical function of demonstrating that the needs and vulnerabilities of the offender have been fully investigated, and that proper attention has been given to her mental and moral well-being. Such paternalistic supervision has always been regarded as particularly important in relation to females and juveniles. As one elderly woman magistrate remarked, (with a kindliness that could hardly be taken as sinister):

> 'Of course they're not mentally ill, but I'd hate anyone to think that I ever sent one to prison without finding out what's been going on in her mind. It's a question of being seen to care and seen to do the thing properly. It's a public responsibility, because these girls aren't in a position to look after their own interests. We have to be very careful with these girls. As a woman I think it matters, I really do.'

This sense of a special responsibility to investigate the mental conditions of female offenders is apparently shared and endorsed by the official policies of the criminal justice system. The Report on Mentally Abnormal Offenders[1] produced by the official government committee headed by Lord Butler, mentions females in general as one of the 'special' categories of offender for whom pre-sentence reports would, ideally, *always* be prepared. It goes on to suggest that since financial exigencies prevent this ideal, all females risking terms of imprisonment should at least be 'screened' by probation officers, who should pay particular heed to the possibility of mental abnormality. The concern that underlies these recommendations is echoed in several of the official policy guidelines concerning the preparation of medical and social reports.[2] These repeatedly suggest that for female offenders pre-sentence reports should be prepared in all but the most routine of cases.

In summary, the selection of male and female offenders for psychiatric examination is typically based upon different criteria of pathology and different expectations of psychiatric help. The selection of male offenders is relatively narrow, and based largely on conspicuous behavioural signs. The female selection is wider, including many whom criminal justice agents do not regard as really 'disturbed', but who appear to have problems that a psychiatrist might be able to clarify. There is already, by this stage, a sexual disproportion in the number of cases 'made available' for professional psychiatric assessment. But on this basis there is as yet no immediate reason to predict any excess of women amongst those who will eventually be psychiatrically *diagnosed*, since it is typically the *male* offenders who are at this stage perceived as the 'real mental cases', and who appear the more disordered and disorderly. As I shall now discuss, however, at the point when psychiatry takes over the assessment a rather different set of concepts and preoccupations are called into play – sometimes to the bewilderment of criminal justice personnel, and often to their chagrin.

The professional diagnosis

The overall outcome of this second round of assessment may be summarized from the outset. In the course of the professional medical investigation the population of female cases (already somewhat inflated by the tendency of criminal justice agents to refer female offenders almost 'on spec'), is allowed to remain disproportionately large, through a parallel readiness of the doctors to describe these women's difficulties in terms of some vague or specific diagnosis. Conversely, the corresponding population of male offenders, (already rather restricted by the judicial tendency to confine male referrals to cases of stereotypical 'madness'), is further pruned by a widespread refusal of doctors to confirm these lay assessments.

The first of these two processes passes relatively unremarked. Where a woman appears relatively 'normal' to the court, the application of a medical diagnosis may occasionally excite surprise or even scepticism but if so, it poses no problems since the sentencer is always free to ignore it. More commonly, the diagnosis of some minor disorder merely satisfies the court's perception of female offenders as having 'problems'. Even if no specific treatment is offered, the diagnosis may give welcome support for the imposition of a lenient or rehabilitative sentence; and if the doctors *are* willing to offer treatment, then even the flimsiest of diagnoses will usually be accepted. The following comments are from a medical text on the preparation of psychiatric reports:

> Many psychiatrists have an image of the magistrate as essentially punitive, while experience shows that they are usually only too happy to accept a recommendation, medical or social, which has a reasonable chance of being constructive. There should be no hesitation in setting up a provisional plan, and

presenting it to the court. Where a court was told that provisional arrangements had been made for an exhausted middle-aged woman thief to spend two weeks in a convalescent home at the seaside, the Court accepted it at once, and sent a message of thanks.

(Gibbens, 1981, p. 253)

The problems start from the opposite direction. There are many offenders (the majority of them male) whom the courts confidently identify as 'mental cases', but whom psychiatrists firmly decline to diagnose, let alone to treat. Again, of course, this is in sharp contradiction to the popular belief that it is psychiatrists who seek to canvass the medical approach and legal personnel who resist it. Instead the number of medical diagnoses falls far short of the expectations of the courts, and even where doctors feel constrained to apply *some* form of diagnosis, there is often a conspicuous reluctance to name any of the categories of disorder that imply any obligation to offer immediate medical treatment.

Psychiatric discourse is diagnostically flexible. The same basis of medical evidence (in terms of what the subject says or does or presents as 'symptoms') can provide grounds for several different diagnoses or for none. This flexibility gives doctors the ability to manipulate the diagnosis, so as to produce a convenient 'fit' between the category into which the subject is placed and the form or degree of involvement which doctors wish to offer. It is this that permits both the curiously liberal application of medical diagnoses in female cases and the far more restrictive pattern in male cases. The remainder of this chapter seeks to expose the precise tactics of medical argument that are involved here. This exposition is based on the analysis of the 187 medical reports collected in the course of this study.[3]

Psychopathy/personality disorder

These two diagnoses play a central part in each of the moves that I shall be discussing. As clinical diagnoses they are closely related, and the various tactics that involve them all depend on the tactical exploitation of the ambiguities in their meanings. Medical discourse finds it convenient to leave these ambiguities unresolved, but analytically it may be helpful to make them explicit.

Historically, the classification of psychopathy predates that of personality disorder. It emerged towards the end of the nineteenth century, as a diagnostic label which was applied to certain troublesome individuals whose mental state lacked the manifest derangements of formal insanity, but whose behaviour, emotions and motivations still seemed outrageously abnormal. The close association between this diagnostic category and antisocial conduct has always made it a highly significant classification for forensic psychiatry. In relation to psychiatry as a whole, however, its medical status has always been peripheral and somewhat suspect. Like its genealogical forbears, 'manie sans délire and 'moral' or 'virtual' insanity, psychopathy has always been located at an uncertain boundary between normality and pathology. It is a condition of pathology yet one which inheres only in the degree of deviation along a continuous spectrum that includes psychological normality; as it was described in 1895 by the first author to adopt the term in its modern sense,[4] psychopathy is 'a morbid variety of the normal'.

Both the specific marginality of the diagnosis, and the ambiguity as to its precise scope, are crucial to all the curious possibilities of its deployment. In its most familiar and uncontested usage, the diagnosis of psychopathy is applied to subjects who appear cognitively normal but who repeatedly behave in exceptionally violent or sadistic ways; who express no convincing remorse for their behaviour;[5] who do not seem to be deterred by normal sanctions; and who do not form normal emotional attachments. In this popular sense of the term, the diagnosis of psychopathy is what lends medical legitimacy to the claim: 'Anyone who can behave like that just has to be *sick*.'

But there is also a less extreme and specific usage of the term, whose origins can be traced to that general medicalization of crime that was taking place around the 1930s. In this model the classification of psychopathy is extended to a whole range of personal deviations, of whom the familiar 'aggressive psychopath' manifests only one variety. Equally important to this schema is the 'inadequate psychopath'. This is an infinitely milder character whose pathology is to be found not in persistent violence but in persistent *failure*: in relationships, or work, or sex, or domesticity, *or medical treatment, or crime.*

The narrow sense of psychopathy allows the medicalization of serious violence, and the wider sense allows the medicalization of deviance in general. This was always a controversial trend, and in recent years it has been repeatedly challenged by the critics of psychiatry, and increasingly disfavoured even within psychiatry itself.[6] One outcome of this has been a patchy but significant movement towards reassigning the category of 'psychopathy' under the seemingly less contentious title of 'personality disorder'. (In the United States, a similar trend has been marked by the substitution of the term 'sociopath'.) The classification of 'personality disorder' is closely related to that of psychopathy, (to which, indeed, it owes most of its characteristics), but it embodies two important differences.

First, the category of personality disorder is intentionally less medical in its connotations. In practice the two classifications relate to the much the same territory of personal abnormality, at the margins of the psychiatric domain. The classification of psychopathy was developed in an attempt to annexe these abnormalities to psychiatry, and thence to a clinical domain of medical disease. The alternative classification of personality disorder was intended to sever that medical connection, by asserting the continuity of these abnormalities with the broader realm of personal variation. The distinction is significantly reflected in the wording of the Mental Health Act, which makes no mention of personality disorder, but includes psychopathy amongst the four categories of legally recognized mental disorder.

Second, the particular construction of the category of personality disorder allows it the potential to be broader in its scope than even the extended classification of psychopathy. The psychological concept of 'personality' is so capacious that there are few attributes of normal or abnormal subjectivity to which it cannot be extended. Correspondingly, there are few personal failings that could not in principle be designated as 'disorders' of personality. Beneath this voluminous diagnostic blanket one can thus find whole armies of ill-assorted bedfellows: the forgettable legions of ordinary misfits; the occasional, infinitely memorable individuals, like the mute, reclusive, identical sisters, with their private rituals and their predilection for arson;[7] even such notorious miscreants as the suburban householder who liked to cut up his acquaintances and flush them down the toilet.[8]

If (as some have recommended) the replacement of the clinical 'psychopathy' by a non-clinical 'personality disorder' had been systematic and uniform, the net change in the diagnostic field would ultimately have been both logical and circumscribed. Certain previously medicalized conditions, already somewhat marginal to medicine, would have been eased out into an alternative and non-medical domain of pathological personality, whilst certain other troubles, previously undistinguished by formal classification, might have found themselves eligible for this new title of pathology. This is not, however, what has happened.

Instead of effecting a secession from the medical project, the category of personality disorder has in fact been partially incorporated into medical discourse. As Carlen has argued,[9] the understanding of personality disorder as a 'non-medical' categorization is always significantly ambiguous. Medical discourse allows it to operate as a kind of anti-diagnosis: a condition of recognizable pathology, but one that is excluded from the medical domain. At the same time, however, medical discourse treats the exclusion as discretionary, tactical, and reversible. Whilst deploying the category as a device for freeing medicine from any particular *responsibility* for the disorders in question, psychiatry has none the less reserved to itself the *expertise* of these conditions, along with the right to diagnose them, to pontificate on them, and also (but entirely at medical discretion) to define them as appropriate for psychiatric intervention. Furthermore, instead of simply replacing the diagnosis of psychopathy, the category of personality disorder has settled down into an uneasy coexistence alongside it, remaining conceptually distinct, yet sharing at least some of the same ground. And an assortment of attempts either to align the two or to construct some logical relationship between them has merely compounded the situation. All that has resulted is an entrenchment of the two categories in a series of conflicting semantic arrangements, of which several have achieved a recognizable currency, but none an unchallenged orthodoxy.

These conceptual alternatives establish the possibility for a variety of diagnostic moves. At one moment, personality disorder can be treated as the general category, with psychopathy as a specific or particularly extreme subspecies of it. On this basis one could logically assume that all psychopaths are by definition personality disordered, although not all who are personality disordered may be properly labelled as psychopaths. At another moment, the categories can be treated as synonymous, so that whoever is cast as either of them may also, by definition, be cast as the other. This assimilation has a dual aspect. From one perspective it can imply that psychopathy and personality disorder are the same, but that in effect this entity is psychopathy: medical, tantamount to madness, and justifying psychiatric intervention. From the other, it can imply that psychopathy and personality disorder are one, but that in effect this entity is personality disorder: non-medical, proximate to normality, and an improper object for medical interference. As I shall now go on to illustrate, these various ambiguities make possible a series of diagnostic manoeuvres which play a crucial part in the medical differentiation of male and female offenders.

A doorway out, a doorway in

'No matter how disturbed they are, when I see the words "personality disorder" in a psychiatric report, I know the doctor's just shown them the door.'

(Stipendiary magistrate)

In the first of these semantic arrangements, the terms psychopathy and personality disorder are used to designate two nested but differently bounded fields of disorder, in which the term psychopath is reserved for only a small core of very serious cases. On this basis, medical reports on male offenders frequently contain statements to the effect that whilst the offender can be properly described as *personality disordered*, his condition is not so serious as to warrant the more serious diagnosis of *psychopathy*. This usage preserves the popular understanding of the term psychopath, and the juxtaposition of the two terms allows psychiatry to draw a meaningful distinction between severe abnormalities and inconsequential ones. But it also provides the conditions for a rather more artful move. It allows the psychiatrist to take a subject who has appeared to the court to be possibly or manifestly 'abnormal'; to circumvent any dispute over this perception, by acknowledging that the subject is disordered; yet then to disclaim any grounds on which the subject should be made a medical responsibility. 'If he had happened to be a psychopath then of course we would accept responsibility', the argument disarmingly implies. 'But actually to be precise he *isn't quite that bad*, so regrettably we are unable to help':

An unstable neurotic individual who has a degree of personality deviation. This combination of traits is exemplified by his unstable mood, his unstable marital history, his abuse of alcohol, particularly when under stress, and his long criminal record. However I do not consider that he falls into any of the categories of mental disorder as defined and described in the Mental Health Act 1959, so could not myself recommend a disposal under that Act.

> (Psychiatric report, case 127, male convicted of arson
> and assault occasioning actual bodily harm)

As defined and described in the Mental Health Act, psychopathy is:

> A persistent disorder or disability of mind (whether or not including significant impairment of intelligence) which results in abnormally aggressive or seriously irresponsible conduct on the part of the person concerned.

Had the doctor *wished* to make a diagnosis on the man described above, even the material he includes in this description would probably have been sufficient to sustain a diagnosis of psychopathy on grounds of mental disability ('an unstable neurotic individual') coupled with abnormal irresponsibility. And when one considers this subject's additional history of aggression, (left unmentioned in this report although common knowledge in relation to the facts of the case), the doctor's reported failure to find adequate evidence for the diagnosis may seem increasingly disingenuous. Here is the official summary of the same case, prepared by the clerk of court:

> Defn. punches his wife, hits her with a kettle, pours hot water over her, attempts to strangle her with a dog lead. She suffers cut over left eye, minor facial scalds and a fractured nose. Defn. himself phones for police. In attempting to resist arrest, defn. pushes a PC, pulls his hair and drags him to the ground, where a struggle takes place. He then voluntarily ceases to struggle. But then jumps from a first-floor balcony and escapes. Later that evening he sets fire to the house, which he admits to the police.

> (Case Summary, case 127, male accused of arson,
> and assault occasioning actual bodily harm)

The 'restrictive' model of the relationship between personality disorder and psychopathy depends upon the understanding that only certain very extreme and probably very specific disorders of personality are sufficient to merit the title 'psychopathy'. The issue of *how* extreme remains unspecified, and in any case this assessment necessarily remains a matter of inscrutable clinical judgment. This usage provides one of the most significant moves whereby conspicuously 'abnormal' offenders can be sent back by psychiatrists as having nothing medically the matter. In the cases examined, this move was entirely restricted to cases involving males. In female cases, a rather different move tended to be used, which depended, as I shall now describe, on an alternative understanding of the relationship between the two terms.

As mentioned before, medical discourse reserves the option of treating the term personality disorder as effectively coextensive with that of psychopathy, thus making the two diagnoses logically reversible. Using this model, whatever can be said of one can also be said of the other; whoever can be described as personality disordered can also be described as psychopathic. In this way, the scope of the diagnosis 'psychopathy' becomes almost infinitely extensible. Almost *any* offender might be described as in some way personality-disordered, and through the tactical assimilation of the two terms, almost any offender can then, if the doctor sees some advantage, be drawn into a diagnosis that even satisfies the strict requirements for a hospital order. The following report is unusually explicit about this move:

> Pauline has lived an unstable and volatile lifestyle. She is someone who has difficulty in maintaining a stable relationship with caring agencies and there are frequent episodes of crisis in her life. The only clearly established aspect of her psychiatric history is that through her early experiences her personality at present shows evidence of immaturity, *therefore in respect of suitability for a hospital order, the appropriate mental disorder on which a medical recommendation would be based would be psychopathic disorder.*
>
>   (Psychiatric report, case 49, female convicted of assult; my italics)

The author of this report can afford to be candid about the tactical nature of the diagnosis: at the point when this report was written, it was already agreed by both doctor and sentencer that a psychiatric disposal would be made. The only real question was whether this should be a hospital order under the Mental Health Act, for which the qualifying diagnosis of psychopathy would be required, or a psychiatric probation order, for which the vague 'immaturity of personality' would probably be sufficient. In this case, the decision ultimately settled on an in-patient psychiatric probation order, and the discursive transformation of this woman into a fully-fledged psychopath was therefore not required. The important point is that this final decision by no means rested on any question of whether a diagnosis of psychopathy would be clinically 'correct'. Instead it depended on an entirely pragmatic consideration as to the most convenient method of 'managing' the subject:

> This [the imposition of a hospital order under a diagnosis of psychopathy] presents difficulties both for the patient and for those responsible for her care, in that the ... patient may feel that such an order is akin to receiving an indeterminate sentence and such difficulties do not lead to cooperation in many cases .... The option of a probation order with a condition of treatment allows one to persuade the patient to have in-patient treatment and then supervised follow-up with the possibility, if crises arise, for compulsory readmission under the auspices of the order[10] and with the sanction of the consequences of a breach of the order. The use of this kind of order is something that I have often employed with patients like Pauline .... In short it provides a much more flexible way of managing them.
>
>   (Psychiatric report, case 49 female convicted of assault)

This use of the ambiguity between psychopathy and personality disorder provides a doorway *in* to psychiatric involvement for many marginally disordered female offenders, just as it simultaneously provides a doorway *out* of psychiatric involvement for many quite seriously abnormal male ones. In the majority of cases, the reasons for this sexual specificity are complex and not immediately apparent; they will be examined in more detail in the next chapter. One can identify, however, an interesting subset of these cases, where the sexual bias is specifically and directly related to differences in the conceptions of male and female normality. The following, for example, is from the statutory medical statement concerning a young woman who is about to be made the subject of a compulsory hospital order, under a diagnosis of psychopathy. The official forms ('section papers') that must be submitted in this circumstance require a statement of the evidence on which the qualifying diagnosis has been made:

> INFORMATION TO ESTABLISH A PERSISTENT DISORDER OR DISABILITY OF MIND
> She has shown evidence of disturbed behaviour since school age, at the time truanting frequently, indulging in petty delinquency and being sexually promiscuous. She has been unable to form emotional relationships, and her behaviour has been impulsive and increasingly antisocial. There is also a history of multiple drug use.
>
> (Statutory medical statement, case 34, female convicted of arson)

Educational maladjustment, disorderly behaviour, lack of emotional ties, illicit drug use and sexual activity outside marriage: all of these breach the expectation of conventional femininity, and in a young woman provide evidence that she is a psychopath. In a male, however, they may be acknowledged as socially deviant, but they are still consistent with the expectations of masculine normality, and are therefore treated as no more than ordinary delinquency:

> He attended a school for maladjusted children at the age of eight for three years ... in all he attended three schools but didn't settle down and at the age of twelve was allocated a home tutor ....
> After leaving school he worked as a labourer for four or five months but since that time he has been in constant police trouble and has worked very little ....
> *Drugs* – he admits to smoking marijuana but only on 'certain occasions' ....
> He has a child by a former girlfriend but he does not support either the mother or the child ....
> OPINION: Quinney is a highly delinquent young man, but this does not bring him within any of the categories of mental disorder as defined and described in s 4 of the MHA 1959.[11] I have therefore no medical recommendation to make.
>
> (Psychiatric report, case 73, male convicted of manslaughter)

Reports on males frequently cite histories of criminal delinquency and sexual promiscuity, but hardly ever suggest that these indicate any medical abnormality. A woman who manifests such traits, however, may be labelled as a psychopath. Prostitution is frequently pathologized in *either* sex, but in female cases even financially unmotivated behaviour can be treated as suspect. One report on a twenty-five year old woman cites as evidence of psychopathy that none of her sexual liaisons has endured beyond two years –

a criterion which few young psychiatrists would like turned against themselves! Similarly, it is only in female cases that a poverty of close friendships and family ties is taken as evidence of psychopathy, although it would seem from the reports that such isolation is typical of both male and female offenders.

The mental illnesses

> The diagnosis [of mental illness] to a great extent determines the recommendation. Having made a diagnosis of mental illness, the examining psychiatrist is under a professional (and perhaps a moral) obligation to offer treatment .... The cynic might observe that by emphasizing one aspect or another of the diagnostic picture, the psychiatrist can manipulate the ... case, and thereby alter his professional obligation.
>
> (Chiswick *et al.*, 1984, p. 88)

Of all the diagnoses that the forensic psychiatrist might make, that of mental illness is the most unambiguously 'medical', and the one where there is the strongest obligation to offer treatment. Other diagnoses, such as mental subnormality or even psychopathy, leave scope for a degree of negotiation and buck-passing: in these cases both the problem and the proper treatment can be redefined as more social or educational than medical. But the psychiatrist cannot argue that mental illness is other than a psychiatric responsibility without undermining the very credibility of psychiatry. An unfortunate effect of this is that the forensic psychiatrist who (for whatever reason) does *not* want to recommend treatment to a particular subject will go to considerable lengths to frame the medical report in terms which avoid suggesting that the subject is actually mentally *ill*.

The simplest tactic here is simply to omit any clinical information that might otherwise indicate such a condition. This is a straightforward tactic, (and one that is certainly used), but it is also a somewhat risky one. If other agents subsequently inform the court of matters which the doctor has conveniently suppressed, then an embarrassing question mark may be placed over the doctor's competence or even integrity:

> BARRISTER: 'I do not need to go into all the details, but as your Lordship can see, that whereas he may be a very competent psychiatrist – and there is no reason to suppose that he is not – what he repeats as having been told to him is in sharp contradiction to the behaviour of the woman at the scene when the fire brigade arrived and it is in stark contradiction to the interview that she had with the police .... When Dr Rothchild saw her a week later – you can see the penultimate paragraph of his medical report – he says she told her story in a clear and rational manner, and he goes on to say "She did not show any evidence of thought disorder, pressure of speech" and so on .... Well, it seems that she was seen by a variety of people. I have been shown a copy of the Social Enquiry Report, which says that her conversation was rambling and

fragmentary, it was difficult to focus her attention and there were various delusions and symptoms of paranoia ...'

(Crown Court transcript, case 26, woman accused of arson)

As a means of manipulating the diagnosis, a safer tactic is to *acknowledge* the embarrassing symptoms, but renegotiate their *meanings*, so that they no longer need imply that the subject is mentally ill. In some mental illnesses, such as depression or anxiety neurosis or hypomania, the symptoms may be seen as simply an extreme version of emotions that can otherwise occur normally. In these cases the pathological meaning of symptoms may be neutralized simply by quibbling over the precise point at which the extreme becomes 'pathological', and drawing the line so that the subject falls outside it. This, for example, is the standard way in which depressive symptoms are dealt with in male cases.

Loosely 'depressive' symptoms, (ranging from simple withdrawal and dejection to serious suicide attempts), are apparently common among offenders. They are mentioned in the majority of reports on female cases and about a third of those on males.[12] In female cases, these were routinely identified as evidence of the illness 'depression', and the majority of psychiatric disposals were for women suffering from depressive disorders of one kind or another. In male cases, by contrast, such potentially pathological features were almost invariably mentioned only casually, and explained, if at all, simply as a normal reaction either to life in general or to the particular strains of the trial or the remand. Even where male offenders manifested such extreme symptoms that medical steps (including anti-depressant drug treatment) had to be taken to relieve them, these symptoms were routinely dismissed as merely 'reactive to the situation and not uncommonly seen in such cases'.[13] On their own they were never treated as grounds for suggesting a psychiatric disposal.

With psychotic symptoms on the other hand, the doctor who wishes to avoid diagnosing mental illness will need to adopt a rather more sophisticated tactic. The offender may be hallucinating, or deluded, or thought-disordered – symptoms that are rather harder to assimilate to normality. But again, the accommodating category of personality disorder is conveniently to hand. In these cases, the 'non-medical' status of personality disorder can again be invoked, thus allowing the symptoms in question to be channelled *out* of medical significance. The heart of the argument is that symptoms which in people of normal personality would only appear in the presence of mental illness, might be manifest by the personality-disordered *even in the absence of mental illness*. Identifying the subject as personality-disordered allows the seemingly pathological symptoms to be mentioned and acknowledged, but then immediately discounted. Self-mutilation and overdose; hyperactivity and catatonia; statements indicating paranoid delusions, hallucinations and thought disorder: all of these symptoms were attributed to personality disorder in one or more of the cases that I examined.

The reports offer various explanations for the appearance of such symptoms in subjects with personality disorder. One is that the personality disordered subject may straightforwardly *simulate* such symptoms, for reasons of his own.[14] Another is that the symptoms may be genuine but that they only arise because of the subject's poor capacity for dealing with ordinary problems. The symptoms thus comprise only 'a transient episode ... reactive to situational stress; such episodes are seen from time to time in people who suffer from severe personality disorder'.[15] The theoretical distinction between a psychotic 'episode' and a psychotic 'illness' seems rather nebulous, especially since all the major mental illnesses are typically episodic in their course. What *is* clear, however, is that where the term 'episode' appears, any apparent derangement of the subject is not going to be taken too seriously.

This reassignment of 'mental illness' as 'personality disorder' allows the forensic psychiatrist not only to neutralize the offender's present symptomatology, but also to cast doubt over the clinical correctness of any previous medical history. Thus it is not uncommon for offenders with well-documented psychiatric histories to be suddenly prised out of this status and reassigned, for the purposes of the court report, to a category of psychiatric normality. One such case involved a middle-aged librarian with a seven-year history of schizophrenia. During a brief period when he had stopped receiving medication for this condition, he attacked a vicar whom he believed to be 'controlling the way a group of people were behaving', and was subsequently convicted of assault occasioning actual bodily harm. The offender is described in the report as 'vague', 'emotionally flattened', 'obsessional', 'expressing grandiose delusions', 'confused' and 'evasive'. Having determined that the man has an abnormal personality, however, the doctor now blandly concludes that 'there appeared to be no evidence of current or past psychotic phenomena'.[16]

In another case, a remand prisoner's peculiar behaviour whilst in the prison hospital led eventually to his transfer on bail to an ordinary psychiatric hospital, where he was diagnosed as schizophrenic and treated with the corresponding medication. Seven months later his mental condition, although still unstable, had in general improved (as would be typical of a treated schizophrenic). The court then requested an updated medical report, with a view to reaching a decision on disposal. The doctor conducting the assessment concedes that the improvement is marked, but concludes, by an extraordinary somersault of reasoning, that:

> This change [is to be seen as] evidence of an abnormal personality (hysterical personality disorder). ... *There is no evidence to suggest that Mr Samuels was suffering from mental illness* .... He is a man who since early adolescence has shown evidence of emotional instability and immaturity of his personality .... It seems clear that his emotional involvement has at times been too much for his unstable personality, and has led to minor psychotic episodes, as has the stress of imprisonment.

(Psychiatric report, case 114, male convicted of theft; italics added)

Although this tactical refusal of the diagnosis of mental illness does sometimes occur in female cases,[17] it is a stratagem of 'anti-diagnosis' which is far more characteristic of males. (The only exceptions in my own sample both involved lesbians convicted of homicide, and in both cases there were also many other features of their treatment which differed sharply from that of heterosexual women).[18] A significant subgroup amongst the males being dealt with in this fashion were several chronic and socially deteriorated schizophrenics.[19] None of these were offered psychiatric disposals, and most of them were eventually subjected to normal tariff sentences, despite the misgivings of the sentencer. These pathetic and unwanted characters make up a considerable proportion of the 'stage army' of mentally abnormal recidivists. Their repetitive circulation through the criminal justice system has been widely documented,[20] and is a matter of constant irritation to criminal justice personnel.[21] From a lay perspective, there is no disguising the psychopathology of these offenders, even if the ingenuity of psychiatrists succeeds in barring them from hospital care.

Diagnosis and disposal

The assessments that I have discussed in this chapter comprise two of the rounds of decision making that must precede any psychiatric disposal. In the first, the offender is identified by the court as requiring psychiatric assesment, and in the second the offender is psychiatrically examined and a report is prepared for the court. As I have described, there are sexual biases in both of these processes, which in both cases serve to restrict the medical involvement with male offenders, whilst allowing a more liberal medicalization of females.

There are a few cases, both male and female, where the decision on disposal appears to be based entirely on these two rounds of assessment. In these cases the agreement that the offender is mentally disordered appears to be constituted as the single and sufficient reason for a psychiatric disposal. Invariably these are cases where mental illness has been diagnosed, and where the offender is still regarded as 'ill' at the point when the sentence is passed. Included here are certain of the more spectacularly psychotic of male offenders,[22] as well as a number of more humdrum female ones, who received a variety of diagnoses including depressive illness and puerperal psychosis.

From the perspective of many of the court personnel, these instances represent the correct and exemplary handling of 'mental cases'. The offender is noted to be disordered by criminal justice personnel; this observation is confirmed by a professional diagnosis; a medical disposal is arranged without further dispute. Even where mental disorder is unambiguously diagnosed, however, this kind of approach is actually far from typical: the question of treatment is rarely presented as solely dependent on the clinical condition of the offender, and, as I discussed in the previous chapter, there is nothing in the formal provisions for psychiatric disposal which suggests that this *should* be the only consideration to be raised at this point. In the majority of cases, the decision-making process moves on from these initial two steps to a further round of alternative or additional deliberations, which will take into account that complex of moral, practical and institutional considerations that I outlined in the last chapter. In the course of this final stage of decision, many offenders who have emerged from these first two rounds with some kind of medical diagnosis will find themselves none the less excluded from a psychiatric disposal, whilst a few others, who in these first two rounds failed even to pass the qualifying test of mental disorder, will be brought back into the process of medicalization.

Notes

1 Butler (1975, para 11.4).

2 See Home Office Circulars 17/1963; 29/1971, 7f, 14d, 37d.

3 Appendix B, Table 2, gives brief details of the reports available in each case, of the statements of pathology contained within them, and of any diagnoses made.

4 Moebius, P., quoted in Mayer-Gross *et al.* (1960, p. 160f).

5 See Case 80, discussed in the penultimate section of Chapter 3.

6 See Ramon (1968) in Miller and Rose, (eds) (1986).

7 This case was dramatized in the BBC documentary *The Silent Twins*, shown on 20.1.86. See also Wallace, 1986. A quite similar case, involving personality disordered identical twins is described in detail in *The Sunday Times* (colour supplement) 28.6.81.

8 The notorious Denis Nilsen case: see *The Times*, 30.10.83; *The Guardian*, 16.11.83.

9 Carlen (1983, p. 195f).

10 This slip of the pen is perhaps significant: technically, compulsory treatment is *not* an option under a psychiatric probation order, although under the circumstances, and given the likely consequences of a refusal to accept treatment, the 'voluntary' nature of the treatment is sometimes more symbolic than real.

11 See s 1 of the 1983 Act. The new Act defines the mental disorders rather differently from the old, but appears to have effected no substantive change in the terms in which doctors reason about the diagnoses concerned.

12 See Appendix B, Table 2.

13 The conceptual distinction between 'reactive' and 'endogenous' depression, and its significance for the outcome of the case, is discussed further in the next chapter.

14 e.g. Cases 115, 119, in both of which the offender exhibited disturbed and bizarre behaviour in prison, including the kinds of 'posturing' sometimes seen in catatonic disorders, and reported auditory hallucinations like those commonly reported in schizophrenia.

15 Psychiatric report, case 1.

16 Case 126.

17 e.g. Case 1. There are, indeed, even some *women* 'whom nobody wants', as described in Carlen (1983, p. 193f). Their problems are extreme, but outside the

scope of this study. In a sense, this book is concerned with the opposite phenomenon – that of how in all but these most extreme of cases, the responsible agencies do continue to 'want' disordered female offenders, even where male offenders in comparable circumstances would be definitely unwanted.

18 Cases 1, 2, 3, 52. The position in which all these lesbian women were placed by the psychiatric reports seems to embody many of the least fortunate aspects of both female and male cases. They are pathologized but not exempted from blame, either legally or morally. They are diagnosed as disordered but refused medical help. Their crimes are treated as evidence of their disturbance, but still dealt with (unlike the vast majority of female offences) by means of severe custodial sentences.

19 Two directly contradictory lines of reasoning are available here, to cover the contingencies of virtually any case: the mental illness can be discounted either because it was *preceded* by evidence of abnormal personality, in which case it is 'merely secondary to the personality disorder', or else because the mental illness has now been 'superseded' by the personality disorder, in which case the mental illness is no longer deemed amenable to treatment.

20 See Lawson (1966); Gibbens *et al.* (1981); Scull (1977).

21 See Loucas (1980, p. 135); Orr (1978); Carlen (1986).

22 e.g. Cases 84, 89, 95, 96.

Chapter six:

Treatment versus punishment

The medical officer may express his opinions frankly but should be careful to give reasons for these opinions. He may indicate medical treatment which, in his view, could usefully be given to an offender, though care should be taken that the report is not made in a form which suggests that the proper treatment of the offender will be the only consideration in the Court's mind.

(Home Office Guidelines on Medical Reports, June 1981/192, 8b1 (33))

Those charged with any part in the sentencing process are faced with the need to combine humanity and compassion with a clear recognition that sentencing is not, in the ultimate analysis, a kind of general welfare service, but is essentially an integral part of criminal justice.

(Hines, 1982, para 16.1)

In the Home Office guidelines, psychiatrists are pointedly reminded that the decision on sentence cannot hinge exclusively on the wellbeing of the offender. The same point is stressed in the professional handbook for magistrates. In practice, however, these exhortations are unnecessary: medical opinion on the treatment of criminals is in any case alert to moral and practical considerations as well as strictly clinical ones, and the restricted availability of 'welfare' resources (including facilities for psychiatric treatment) ensures that judges and magistrates rarely have the *opportunity* to prioritize this aspect. This chapter is concerned with all the 'other' considerations, apart from those of the offender's medical condition, that influence the decisions of doctors and sentencers.

The morality of subjects

Despite the distinction that is commonly drawn between punitive and rehabilitative sentencing, there is a conceptual continuity in the decisions that are involved. The arguments for either type of disposal are typically dictated by the same moral economy of 'just deserts'. Thus the more blameworthy the offender, the more insistent will be the demands for punishment, and the less appropriate it will seem to grant the comparative benefits and exemptions of a rehabilitative disposal. Conversely, the decision to permit such a disposal often depends less on the suspension of moralistic reasoning, that on the conclusion that the offender does not, (given all the circumstances), deserve to be punished, and does deserve special compassion and help. From both the judicial and the medical perspective, such moral reasoning can play a crucial part in determining whether the offender will be judged suitable for a psychiatric disposal.

On the judicial side, the demand for such calculation is explicit in the provisions of the Mental Health Act. In assessing the suitability of a hospital order, the court is required to 'have regard to all the circumstances including the nature of the offence and the character and antecedents [i.e. criminal record] of the offender'. As is evidenced in various Appeal Court Rulings,[1] this injunction allows sentencers to declare a medical disposal unsuitable in cases where the subject appears morally culpable, intractably criminal, or personally undeserving – even if there are obvious medical grounds on which a hospital order could be imposed. The same moral reasoning also influences medical decisions, as is noted rather defensively in the following extract from a recent textbook of forensic psychiatry:

> The NHS consumes a vast amount of the nation's wealth ... its financial resources are limited, however, and it follows that there must be a system of priorities. Without putting too fine a point on things, the law abiding citizen expects that his or her needs shall take priority over those of a group of individuals whose behaviour is reprehensible, and who do not rate very highly in the public eye. This of course is human nature, and it is unwise to ignore public feeling.
>
> (Lawson, W., in *Craft and Craft* 1984, p. 173)

Predictably, these moral calculations will impact differently on male and female cases. The differences in the assumptions about male and female natures that were discussed earlier in relation to legal guilt and the verdict, operate equally powerfully in the assessment of the offender's 'just deserts' at the point of sentencing. They influence what moral meanings are attached to both the crime and the offender, and can modify the moral significance of a diagnosis of disorder.

The 'disappearance of action' from the reports on female offenders will obviously be advantageous to the assessment of their moral character. In the extreme instance, the woman's discreditable behaviour can be so completely obscured in these documents that there seems nothing left to excite any moral opprobrium. One of the reports on a woman charged with murdering her boyfriend,[2] for example, succeeds in omitting all direct reference to the killing itself or to the financial argument that preceded it. With these unfortunate details apparently forgotten, the field is cleared for a glowing report on the woman's gentleness and goodness:

> A twenty-three-year-old slightly built woman who ... has always cherished an ambition to be involved in one of the caring professions. She ... has had only one boyfriend, [i.e. her victim] who, in spite of his persistent abuse of her, has been the only person she has ever loved. She has borne him two children; has always felt guilty about not being married to him. At the time of his death she was breastfeeding their three-month-old infant. She appears still to be emotionally involved with him and in spite of his violence towards her, claims she has no feelings of hatred .... A small, mild woman ... a good mother to her children ... a warm, likable person, very easy to talk to, and with many good, caring qualities.
>
> (Psychiatric report, case 22, woman accused of murder)

On the basis of this commentary, the woman's moral character seems spotless. To suggest that there is anything for which she deserves punishment must seem either redundant or churlish. On the contrary, there is much for which she deserves compensation:

> This woman has suffered considerably during her relationship with [her boyfriend], and has suffered a great deal of mental anguish since his death. In my opinion the events of that night will leave scars on her far worse than those of any physical injury she has received .... I suggest that she will need a great deal of help and support over the next few weeks, in terms of rehabilitation into society.
>
> (ibid.)

What is therefore presented as the just deserts of this woman is a complex programme of social rehabilitation, economic support, accommodation, probationary support and psychotherapy. There is no suggestion that the woman is or ever has been mentally disturbed; the offer of psychotherapy appears to be a token of sympathy for her bereavement.

Even where the discreditable details of a female crime *are* directly addressed, the ambiguous construction of female responsibility may allow the formal acknowledgement of the woman's legal guilt to be undercut by the refusal of any moral guilt. This is a situation which is uncomfortable to judicial reasoning, especially if the offence itself is of such gravity that the sentence would normally be a severe one. For most practical purposes, the perception of the 'justice' of criminal sentencing depends on a taken-for-granted correspondence between legal and moral guilt. It is the technicality of legal guilt that grounds the initial conviction, but it is moral gult that justifies the imposition of a penalty. The process of mitigation allows minor discrepancies between legal and moral guilt to be taken into account, but the more extreme the gulf between them, the more judicial discourse will be embarrassed by the distinction. If the offender has been found guilty of a serious offence, and yet at the same time is constructed as a subject who cannot rightly be held to blame, then the demands of justice may seem to be equally slighted by a lenient sentence or a severe one. A penalty commensurate with the offence will appear unjust if the offender is construed as morally innocent. A nominal sentence may make a mockery of the finding of legal responsibility, with its technical entailment that the offender was deliberately doing wrong.

In male cases, the assumption of an uncomplicated responsibility for criminal action tends to avert such a situation. But the ambiguous conception of subjectivity that is invoked in female cases constantly threatens the link between legal and moral guilt. The following extract provides a vivid illustration of such a case. The offender, convicted of arson, is a woman of twenty-two, of low intelligence, who has set light to her lodgings after an argument with the manager of the property.

> She knows the nature of her actions, knows that it is wrong to set fires and is aware of the dangers. She has a pleasant and warm personality, and is not by nature a bad person. As to the offences, she tells me that she sets fires when she gets angry. It is known that people with low intelligence are easily frustrated and get angry. She told me she quite likes little fires and doesn't want to cause serious damage. Previously she slashed her wrists on one occasion when she was angry.
>
> There is no evidence of any psychotic illness, or any depression. Nor has there been any evidence of any mental illness either now or in the past. I do not think that she would benefit from any medical treatment and specifically drugs would have little to offer her.
>
> RECOMMENDATIONS: ... I think the danger is that if she is expected to live a normal life now, she would regress into fragmentation. I therefore strongly support any move to keep her in a therapeutic environment. I would respectfully suggest that a custodial sentence might be inappropriate since the girl is not by nature bad, and punishment would have little to offer. The acts were only committed out of misplaced anger and whereas they were serious they were not meant to cause damage. The possibility of a Section 60 order[3] is a real one.
>
> (Psychiatric report, case 32, female convicted of arson)

There was never any question about the woman's legal responsibility: she knew what she was doing, intended to do it, understood the dangers, and knew that it was wrong. But still the report refuses to make her a morally guilty subject. The woman is not 'naturally' bad, but merely afflicted with the disadvantage of low intelligence, and the low threshold of frustration which commonly accompanies this. Her bad behaviours are accordingly 'bracketed off'. They are not part of her proper moral nature, (which is pleasant and warm), and it is therefore not morally right to punish her for them. It is not that the report ascribes her behaviour to any extraneous 'illness': it categorically does *not*. It merely presents them as the comprehensible product of that marginal subjectivity that it attributes to her: amiably amoral, and poised precariously at the very threshold between conscious rationality and a 'regression into fragmentation'.

Having jointly constructed such a subject, neither legal nor medical discourse can think quite how to deal with it. The subject is socially dangerous, medically undiagnosable, criminally convicted but morally unblamable. She both must and must not be treated as responsible. From the legal perspective, the medicalization of the case seems to offer the simplest line of escape from the quandary, even if the medical status of the subject is itself quite problematic. Medical authorities also feel uneasy, but ultimately they adopt the same paradoxical stance. The writer of this report declares that the woman has never been mentally disordered and neither needs nor can benefit from medical treatment. Yet despite this, he rather curiously concludes that 'the possibility of a section 60 [i.e. hospitalization] order is a real one', and that the woman needs residential therapy rather than custodial punishment. The same ambiguous conclusion is endorsed by all the other professionals involved in the case, including probation officers, lawyers, and the other doctors who examine her, even though none of them can bring themselves to declare her mentally disordered. The construction of the case seems to preclude any satisfactory closure. Instead of imposing a sentence, the court therefore keeps remanding the case for further and yet further reports, until eventually, (nine months after the initial conviction), the woman is accepted as a resident in a therapeutic community, and a psychiatric probation order is imposed.

The moral assessment of male cases is very different. In the first place, the emphasis on the external world of male offenders ensures that the crime itself is set in sharp relief, in the full force of its harm or threat: it cannot be allowed to disappear from the assessment of the subject's moral deserts, as it sometimes can in female cases. Furthermore, the characteristic perception of male offenders as inherently intentional, knowing, and rational tends to ensure that the offender appears in the worst possible light in relation to his crimes. Even where a male offender is stated to be mentally disordered, and where the actions in question are directly attributed to his psychiatric condition, the assumption of his moral responsibility for those actions is not necessarily suspended. Take this case of a convicted male arsonist. As a child, this man suffered brain damage, which has resulted in low intelligence and epilepsy. He has also had numerous hospitalizations for depression, and is currently diagnosed as suffering from a 'depressive reaction secondary to personality disorder'. In the report, these clinical details are discussed in some detail, and (as in the female case discussed earlier) the firesetting is attributed to his (organically determined) low stress threshold, and his depressive feelings at the time of the offence. But despite this, the report refuses any concessions to his moral responsibility for the act, remarking only that:

> No evidence of any psychiatric disorder which would interfere with his responsibility were discovered. He does have the personality disorder with some temporal lobe activity, *but he was told this in the past and knows* that he is liable to impulsive behaviour when the stress factors in his life become too high … I am unable to assist the Court with any specific psychiatric recommendations. He is mentally and physically fit for whatever course the Court should wish to take.
>
> (Psychiatric report, case 107, male convicted of arson; italics added)

The assumption that the actions of the male offender will be governed by rationality and knowledge means that his 'knowledge' of his disorder and its likely effects are expected to enable him to exercise a kind of advance responsibility for these tendencies, and somehow to counteract them. Since he has apparently failed to do so, his persistence in impulsiveness is treated as a matter for which he must be held personally responsible. It is not an occasion for medical excuses, and can neither exempt him from blame nor justify a medical disposal. Another psychiatrist, called by the defence, is rather more liberal in his interpretation of the case, and offers in-patient treatment. The court evidently favours the former approach, however, and sentences him to seven years imprisonment.

In the case above, the reports make a point of asserting the offender's responsibility. But the assumption of male responsibility is in any case so deeply rooted that it continues to damn the male offender even at the same moment as he is apparently being described as *not* quite responsible. The following excerpt is from a Social Enquiry Report. The conviction in this case followed an incident in which, having first turned on the gas and doused his surroundings and his clothing with paraffin, the man set fire to himself. His council flat was damaged in the resulting blaze, and he has therefore been prosecuted for arson. The man has a long psychiatric history; his wife had left him some two weeks before the offence; since that time his family have repeatedly restrained him from suicidal behaviour.

> Initially during my contact with Mr Thomas he presented as a manipulative and childish individual, who would often infer that if he was not given immediate help, of the type he requested, he would be driven to another suicide attempt. He was often vague and defensive, and would completely misconstrue information given to him, if it was not what he wanted to hear ....
>
> [Immediately prior to the offence] Mr Thomas's behaviour had altered. He had thrown his grown up children out of the house, and had been making threats to kill his wife. He had apparently visited his general practitioner, and the B Hospital casualty department. Dr Unwin at C Hospital was again contacted and was adamant that she was 'not prepared to accept an inadequate angry arsonist into a mental hospital' ....
>
> He obviously misses his wife badly, but his behaviour is that of a spoilt child trying to regain something he has lost ....
>
> CONCLUSION: I feel that the three-year probation order [imposed for an earlier offence] reinforces Mr Thomas's dependency. He is not psychiatrically ill, and does not need medical treatment. He has to learn to take responsibility for his own decisions .... In my opinion, Mr Thomas's behaviour in the last eight months is part of an irrational attempt to persuade his ex-wife to return to him.
>
> (Psychiatric report, case 99, male convicted of arson)

Here is a man who is described as vague, defensive and consistently misconstruing information; whose suicidal behaviour is interpreted as an 'irrational' attempt to get his wife back; who is repeatedly described as childish and irresponsible. But in the very same breath, the report underwrites the assumption that the subject must still, despite all such contradictory appearances, be regarded as a conscious, rational, self-determining subject, bearing full responsibility for his actions.

If he misconstrues information, it is a *wilful* misconstruction. If he is vague and defensive, or acts irrationally, or claims that he is 'driven' to his extreme acts of self-destruction, this cannot be taken at face value as evidence of any *actual* lack of lucidity or self-determination. Instead it is taken as a perverse form of deliberate intentional activity, as a means of manipulating people. Similarly, his childishness, although repeatedly asserted, is never taken to imply a morally forgivable immaturity, but instead is taken as the wilful and culpable childishness of a perverse adult, who could behave otherwise if he so wished.

These assumptions leave no room for this dangerously self-destructive individual to be offered psychiatric or even probationary 'support'. Such provisions are presented as merely removing the moral responsibility that must belong to the offender himself. This 'must' is both prescriptive and descriptive. Prescriptively it demands that if need be, he will have to be *forced* into a position of responsibility, by the withdrawal or refusal of any props to his dependency. But the notion that the man 'just must' be morally responsible is also *descriptive*. Only by assuming him to be *already* morally responsible does it make sense to blame him for *not* being responsible. Only by assuming him to be already rational does it make sense to suppose that he will desist from irrationality if given rational reason to do so. Only by assuming that he is already self-determining, does it make sense to assume that (if he pleases) he *can* thus desist. It seems to be treated as inconceivable that this man is actually not, beneath all his perversity, a moral clone of the legally rational man. He is sentenced to two years' suspended imprisonment.

The morality of disorders

It is a commonplace of medical sociology that the medicalization of a condition will generally absolve the subject from social blame. Once failures of social functioning have been identified as symptomatic of a medical condition, these failures are no longer treated as a matter for social sanction.[4] At some level it is this principle that can often exempt the mentally disordered from being punished for anti-social behaviour committed whilst 'ill'. This social exemption does not, however, extend equally to all disorders. Most crucially, it may be withheld in cases where the disorder can itself be seen as in some way the offender's own fault. The different conception of action and responsibility in male and female offenders inevitably means that it is male offenders who are most disadvantaged by such reasoning. Thus, for example, the male alcoholic or drug addict will typically be seen as a culpable hedonist, who has brought about his own medical downfall. If he then commits some drug or alcohol related offence, then his medical disorder will bring him little sympathy. His female counterpart, on the other hand, will commonly be viewed as a victim of circumstance or coercion, and if drink or drugs 'drive her to crime', she will be seen as deserving rescue and compassion. This difference in the moral construction of disorders extends beyond these obvious instances, however, to encompass a whole range of conditions where the aetiology of the disorder can in any way be related to the personal or social circumstances of the offender. This is illustrated by the different treatment of 'reactive depression' in male and female cases.

Reactive depression, as understood in mainstream psychiatry, is a disorder of mood, characterized by abnormal feelings of grief, despair, worthlessness and so on. It is often accompanied by disturbances of sleep, activity, libido and appetite, and carries a distinct risk of suicide if left untreated. It is an uncontroversial and frequently diagnosed condition, that differs from the other common category of depressive disorder, 'endogenous depression', both in its particular clinical features, such as the precise pattern of sleep disturbance, and in its presumed aetiology. Endogenous depression is believed to arise spontaneously, from inherent, possibly biochemical, processes. Reactive depression is construed as an excessive, and thus ultimately pathological, reaction to distressing life events and circumstances. In mainstream psychiatry reactive depression is a routinely treated disorder, which often results in voluntary or compulsory hospitalization. It can normally be relieved by a combination of social supports and anti-depressant medication. In its own special treatment of this disorder, however, forensic psychiatry takes up these familiar terms, and by simply twisting them around, is able to produce two subtly different readings of the condition, which justify two contradictory lines of moral assessment.

The first version, which is typical of female cases, differs little if at all from that of mainstream psychiatry. The reasoning starts from the woman's material troubles, moves from these to her inner sufferings, and concludes with an unequivocal assertion of illness. 'This woman's life is full of troubles', the reasoning implies, 'and look, all this suffering has made her ill'. The final emphasis is on her *illness*, and the logical conclusion is that the woman is medically disordered and deserves whatever remedy medicine can offer. As in the following example, the insistence on the moral exemptions of the medical condition is undeterred by the acknowledgement of its origin in the external events of the woman's life, even in her own criminal behaviour. This woman has killed her five-year-old son, following the break-up of her marriage:

> She presents to the staff in the prison a facade of alert preoccupation with the day-to-day affairs of herself and the other inmates. However, this conceals a profound anguish .... She is undoubtedly now suffering from a depressive mental illness which renders her a suicide risk. *This is obviously in part a reaction to her offence.* Her mental state at the material time was quite clearly morbid, *albeit that it was understandably related to the circumstances of her marriage ....* I

am satisfied that at the material time she was suffering from an abnormality of mind (as induced by a depressive reaction amounting to mental illness) ... Mrs Vincent remains ill and a serious suicide risk. I recommend that her case be disposed by means of a hospital order, under the Mental Health Act.

(Psychiatric report, case 16, female convicted of manslaughter by reason of diminished responsibility; italics added)

The alternative reading, which typifies the male cases, moves in the opposite direction. It leaves behind the fact of the illness, and instead focuses back on the material circumstances that have given rise to it. The final statement is of external, social, or material troubles, for which the man himself should take responsibility. 'Yes, he has made himself ill', the logic goes, 'but this is only because of the troublesome life he leads. He has made his bed, now let him lie on it'. Medical remedies can therefore be presented as misplaced, irrelevant, or undeserved:

He still presents as a quiet man, a good historian, who suffers from a depressive illness which is more reactive to environment than to any deep seated clinical origin .... As far as I am aware, there is no treatment for his condition, and I am therefore unable to assist the Court with any specific psychiatric recommendation.

(Psychiatric report, case 109, male convicted of arson)

His depression ... is secondary to the circumstances in which he was living at the time of the offence, without employment, without stable income, without his family and without a proper home. These circumstances were the predictable consequences of his lifelong hedonism and irresponsibility ... [and] his long history of alcohol and drug abuse .... Since his bouts of depression are secondary to his circumstances, further episodes are inevitable unless he gains the motivation to alter his lifestyle, drinking and attitudes. Medical intervention can therefore have little of any significance to offer, and I would not myself make any medical recommendation.

(Psychiatric report, case 117, male convicted of robbery)

The diagnosis of reactive depression, like that of personality disorder, has a Janus-like aspect, guarding a threshold between normality and pathology, and looking simultaneously in both directions. On one side it looks to the normality of human troubles and to the social expectation that subjects will bear responsibility for the course of their own lives. On the other it looks to the pathology of mental reactions that are too violent, too inconsolable or too all-embracing, and by medicalizing this pathology invokes the expectations of moral exemption and social sympathy. Out of such duality, a single diagnosis can again provide the conditions for a two-way traffic between the appropriateness and the inappropriateness of treatment. On one hand it allows certain (mostly female) offenders, who might otherwise seem to be suffering only from the normal wear and tear of unlovely lives to be brought into the fold of psychiatric treatment. And on the other, it allows certain other (mostly male) offenders, who are diagnosed as mentally ill and who might otherwise seem obvious candidates for medical treatment, to be excluded from such measures.

Treatability and the institutional constraints

AUTHOR: What kind of disorder would you tend to regard as most treatable? PSYCHIATRIST: Oh that's a question we're so often asked! [...] I think it's the wrong question. Look. If you mean 'What disorders can I cure?', I'd probably have to say 'None'. [...] If you mean 'What disorders can I give treatment to?' I could say 'All of them'. (It wouldn't necessarily do any *good*, but if you gave me the facilities I could have a go!) But if you mean 'Which disorders can I do some *good* by treating?' well I'd have to say, 'First show me the patient, second tell me what you mean by 'good', third tell me how much time and money and nurses and beds you're going to give me, fourth – and so on'. It's a complete misunderstanding to say 'this disorder is treatable or that one isn't'. I'm constantly trying to get people to understand this.

(Forensic psychiatrist)

In this section, I deal with the institutional aspects of 'treatability'. As the quotation above implies, the question of treatability is as much a political and institutional issue as a theoretical or clinical one, being largely determined by the practical availability of resources and the social objectives that treatment is expected to fulfil. Accordingly, the recent changes in the organization of psychiatry have produced directly corresponding changes in the types of patients who will now be assessed as 'treatable'.

The psychiatric project originally formed itself around the institutional containment of large numbers of socially incompetent and troublesome subjects, in conditions of long-term medical detention.[5] Under the treatment regimes of the large asylums, with their locked wards and physical restraints, there were few practical obstacles to the medicalization of chronically disturbed, dangerous, or refractory offenders. And in a political climate that favoured the permanent segregation of all manner of social misfits, the unlikeliness of improvement was if anything a reason to *favour* the medical approach, with its promise of indefinite detention, rather than to settle for the finite imprisonment that would normally be offered by the penal system. Since the beginning of this century, however, there have been changes in the philosophy and organization of psychiatry that have effectively put paid to this approach. In the process these changes have forced a major redefinition of the groups of people now considered suitable for psychiatric treatment.

The new-look psychiatry has turned its back on the large asylums. It bases itself 'in the community'; it expects hospital admissions to be brief; it emphasizes rehabilitation and social coping; and it makes few provisions for either long-term care of the chronically disordered or secure containment of the dangerous. The incurably incompetent or irremediably dangerous patient is therefore an embarrassing encumbrance to it. Psychiatry in general and forensic psychiatry in particular has responded to this problem by a double redefinition of their populations.

First, there has been the gradual redefinition of the domain of psychiatric disorder, as already outlined in relation to psychopathy. In recent decades, psychiatry has found it increasingly convenient to yield to those critics who have always argued that the medically marginal abnormalities of psychopathy and mental subnormality are actually not psychiatric problems at all, but social, educational, personal or criminological ones. This has allowed psychiatry to pass much of the responsibility for the management of these subjects to the alternative agencies of social work, education, and criminal justice. It has thereby managed to disencumber itself of the two groups of disordered subjects whose needs for long-term supervision and support tend in practice to prove most burdensome – as the alternative agencies are now discovering. This pruning of psychiatric obligations has left it with only the mental illnesses and the residual categories of minor and 'neurotic' disorders. Conveniently, the former of these are the conditions most likely to respond to currently available therapies, especially drugs. The latter, equally conveniently, are the conditions least likely to require intensive supervision or institutional care.

Second, there has been a subtle redefinition of the nature of psychiatric obligation itself. Psychiatry has increasingly rejected the notion of an automatic responsibility for even this more limited medical population, and has abandoned any assumption that the needs of these subjects will necessarily determine what psychiatric facilities will be provided. Instead, psychiatric reasoning now tends to start from the practical provisions which it chooses to make available, and to define the proper population for psychiatric responsibility by reference to these available facilities. It is this that grounds the criterion of 'treatability' that is given such weight in the modern deliberations concerning the appropriateness of medical disposal.[6]

In concrete terms, the current ideal of 'community care' in psychiatry means that mentally disordered people should normally live at home, (or at worst in 'a home': certainly not in hospital). Their occasional visits to out-patient and family practitioner clinics are ideally to be supplemented by contact with social workers, community nurses and voluntary agencies, with back-up from day centres, and other supports from the Social Services. *In extremis*, they can be offered short-term 'crisis' admissions to unlocked psychiatric wards in local general hospitals. These services systematically favour the treatment of those who are perceived either as compliant, competent and harmless enough to remain at large, or else as so temporarily or remediably troublesome that once hospitalized they can soon be discharged again. Such subjects are likely to be judged 'treatable' whether or not their troubles fall into any strictly medical category, and whether or not medical treatment can bring about either full or permanent cure. Conversely, this pattern of provisions disfavours those who are so dangerous that they will need secure provision, or so chronically deranged that they are likely to need long-term containment. Such patients are likely to be assessed as 'untreatable', even if they are undisputedly disordered, and even if treatment might permit some improvement or impede deterioration.

Putting away with a pill

> DEFENCE COUNSEL: 'He's an excitable sort of a man as you can see from the doctor's report'.
> JUDGE: 'Well, he's got to stop getting excited. It's the court's affair to stop him getting excited and put him where the public can be protected'.
> DEFENCE COUNSEL: 'He has this illness and becomes excited. It's not his fault. The doctors hope he will settle down for a passage of time'.
> JUDGE: 'He wants a sedative …. What happens next week? Another Wild West Show? That's what worries me. Something has got to be done about it. Perhaps I should put him somewhere where he can be kept under control or be given a pill. He's been in mental hospital once'.
> (Transcript, male convicted of burglary and criminal damage)

Despite the recent changes in the organization of psychiatry, the conception of a largely custodial mode of psychiatric treatment, justified primarily by the simple fact that the subject is mentally disordered, has never been erased from the expectations of sentencers. As in the case quoted above, this was very often the kind of institutional provision that was envisaged for those 'typical mental cases' who figured so conspicuously in the comments by court personnel. What these officials had in mind for these disorderly men was psychiatric treatment of a primarily sedative nature, entailing secure, preventative, and often long-term hospitalization. The offenders concerned were generally regarded as actually or potentially dangerous, as radically different from 'ordinary' offenders, and generally as unlikely to be curable. It was the humaneness of the incarceration rather than the likelihood of therapeutic improvement that made hospitalization seem the preferable or proper disposal.

Psychiatrists, predictably, were generally less than ready to underwrite such an approach, but it was still conspicuous that the majority of cases where they *did* endorse it were cases involving males.[7] Indeed, whilst only a handful of the female cases recommended for psychiatric disposal were assessed as needing long-term, in-patient care, this was generally seen as imperative for the males. *All* the treatment recommendations for diagnosed male psychopaths, and the majority of recommendations for males suffering *any* form of disorder, suggested that treatment should be under conditions of security. This pattern echoes the overall distribution of disposals that I mentioned at the outset:[8] although males are proportionately under-represented in psychiatric disposals overall, a larger proportion of male psychiatric disposals entail treatment in conditions of secure and indefinite detention. What is more, the serious shortage of such resources means that the number of psychiatric disposals that are actually made falls far short of those that *could* be agreed upon if more facilities were available. There are large numbers of cases, (several of which have become brief *causes célèbres* in the press,[9] but many more of which go unremarked), where mentally disordered offenders are ultimately denied a hospital order simply because no secure hospital place can be found for them. Most of these are cases involving men. Just as it is predominantly males who are seen to *need* such facilities, so it is males who are predominantly disadvantaged by the shortage of them.

This disproportionate demand for secure or long-term facilities for disordered male offenders is not reducible either to differences in the pattern of male and female diagnosis, or to differences in their pattern of offending. Although there *are* male-female disparities in both these parameters, the disparity in the perceived need for secure facilities cuts across both of these.[10] A number of different factors are involved here.

First, the severity of the moral assessment of male offenders means that it is generally only in cases involving quite major disorder that the medical aspects of the case are granted any priority. Male offenders afflicted with more borderline, minor or chronic disorders tend to be screened out of the process of psychiatrization at an early stage, by the more urgent demands of retribution. By default, there is thus a tendency for that population of male offenders for whom treatment *is* regarded as appropriate to be pre-selected towards the more extreme and acutely disturbed cases, for whom, almost by definition, the more restrictive provisions are likely to be regarded as necessary.

Second, and compounding this, minor disorders that might in principle be suitable for treatment in a non-custodial setting are less likely in male cases to be assessed as *remediable* by such treatment. As I shall discuss in a moment, there is less readiness to view disordered male offenders as capable of benefiting from the kinds of low-level support than can be offered in the community: the disorders of male offenders, whether major or minor, tend to be viewed as relatively intractable, except by means of direct restraint. If neither the disorder nor the crime seem grave enough to justify a custodial response (whether medical or penal), there often seems little to be gained by pursuing a psychiatric disposal: it is easier for the court simply to impose a light tariff sentence and be done with it.

Finally, the perceived need for disordered males to be treated in secure conditions is related to the perception of danger. At the crudest level, there is the perception of male offenders as physically harder to restrain than females. (In one notable case,[11] involving a psychotic and suicidal but actually quite cooperative male offender, the only factor cited as significant in deciding between a secure and a non-secure placement was the fact that he held a black belt in karate.) Even without such particular accomplishments, however, there is generally a greater tendency for male offenders to be perceived and identified as 'dangerous', and as therefore requiring a custodial disposal 'in the interests of public safety'[12]. The most seriously violent of disordered males may be seen as untreatable even in the secure conditions of a special hospital,[13] and male offenders with any history of violence are now seldom welcome in the open wards of ordinary hospitals. Even where psychiatrists are themselves willing to risk admitting such an offender, the resistance of hospital managers, nursing staff or trades unions may make it impossible for the admission to be arranged.[14]

Female offenders, however, are almost never regarded in this way: generally they are regarded as requiring no more security than is provided by the average local psychiatric unit. This difference seems unrelated either to the seriousness of their offences or to their past history of violence. Females convicted of homicide, for example, are quite commonly treated either by a psychiatric probation order or by an ordinary hospital order without restriction on discharge; an approach that is almost never adopted with males.[15] The same is true of female offenders with repeated convictions for serious assaults and woundings. One of the cases in my sample involved a woman convicted of causing actual bodily harm,[16] having pulled a door off its hinges and banged it over the head of a boyfriend. The psychiatric report documents a ten-year history of woundings and other violence, including twenty-two separate attacks on strangers, relatives, professional workers, and fellow inmates of hostels and hospitals. In the analysis of the 'essential ingredients' of this case, however, these uncomfortable details suddenly seem to evaporate. The woman is presented as merely 'deprived', 'damaged', 'victimized', and 'insecure'. Her misdemeanours are blandly glossed over as 'a gravitation towards petty criminality' and 'impulsive and irresponsible behaviour', and her (arguably quite appropriate) expressions of guilt and self-denigration are sympathetically pathologized, as evidence of a 'distorted self-image'. Nowhere is there any suggestion that this woman should be regarded as a risk to the public, let alone as too dangerous for admission to hospital. The recommendation of a psychiatric probation order is accepted without demurrer by the court.

Keeping it in the family

'A woman's place is in the home'
(It's like being in a Home)

'Marriage is an institution'
(A total institution)

(Graffiti, ladies' toilet, psychiatric out-patient clinic)

Several sociologists have commented on the greater involvement of 'informal' social controls in the management of female deviance.[17] Put crudely, the argument is that the comparative exemption of women from formal control by the criminal justice system is made possible by their greater subjection to informal controls, especially within the family. Such dynamics are clearly in operation in many decisions to treat female offenders in the community rather than demanding the formal protection of custodial provisions. Within my own sample, there was no case in which a mentally disordered male was regarded as suitably dealt with by being returned to the safe-keeping of his family. In female cases, however, the family was frequently presented as the ideal agency for providing whatever control and surveillance was needed. The following, for example, concerns a schizophrenic and leucotomized woman who has repeatedly threatened to kill her husband and has meanwhile set light to the marital home 'because her husband refused her a cigarette':

> On admission [to prison on remand] she was severely ill, with numerous delusional ideas focusing partly on her relationship with her husband .... She felt that her husband was 'driving her mad' and said that she had wanted to get rid of him .... I think she shows little real understanding of the consequences of her actions ....
>
> I would not feel that her admission to Rampton is justified. For many years she seems to have coped reasonably well when living with her family and having out-patient treatment. She is not imminently dangerous to others at present ... providing that she can have regular psychiatric supervision, I think she could be satisfactorily looked after in the community.
>
> (Psychiatric report, case 35, female convicted of arson)

Differences in the perceived dangerousness of disordered males and females and their perceived need for institutional control are most vividly illustrated in cases involving attacks by parents on their children. Where a father is convicted of harming his children, his continued presence in the family is generally seen as a dangerous liability, and never as a precious benefit to be preserved at all costs. With fathers there is no particular presumption (as there tends to be with mothers) that any violence must spring from mental abnormality but in any case, even where a violent father *is* viewed as mentally disordered, this fact is treated as merely compounding the need to protect the family from his behaviour. Where it is a *mother* who is convicted of harming her children, there is almost invariably a continuing emphasis on retaining the unity of the family and maintaining the maternal relationship. In such cases, the maternal violence will routinely be attributed to psychiatric disorder,[18] but in these cases this condition is seen as a reason for future optimism.

This optimism is not always well founded. My own sample, for example, included two cases in which women had killed their children whilst still receiving 'treatment in the community' as a result of previous attacks on them; in one of these cases, the earlier attack had resulted in a criminal conviction for wounding. The following report offers a typical example of the kinds of reasoning that are involved here. It concerns a woman convicted of causing grievous bodily harm to her eighteen-month-old daughter, whom she has stabbed in the back. Ever since the birth of this child, the mother has been diagnosed as depressed, and has had three periods of hospitalization.

Winnie Young clearly constituted a serious risk to her child. My department was extremely concerned that Winnie might commit suicide or infanticide …. Our obvious aim was to cement as much as posible the mother–child relationship from an early stage for the sakes of both Winnie and the baby, for we have always held the view that the depressive disorder would resolve itself in due course and allow Winnie to return home and care for her baby and her husband. This is, indeed, what happened when she was eventually discharged. She continued to receive support from her husband, her mother, a health visitor and my community nurse colleague. Also her medication continued through my out-patient clinic …. Through the first half of that year she was leading a normal life, caring for her husband, child and home. In early August unfortunately she became depressed again ….

[Following this attack on the child] it is obviously important to have a clear view of the future management. Firstly our aim here is to treat Mrs Young. One would usually then expect her to return home to care again for her family. It is still important that she should be able to re-establish her relationship with her child. It is equally important for the child that this should occur ….

Now that Mrs Young has suffered from at least two severe episodes of psychotic depression, then the risk that she may suffer in the future must be higher than for the average woman. I believe that the risks to her daughter will be minimal once the child can communicate clearly verbally and in particular once she is attending school ….

It is most important that Mrs Young's psychiatric disorder receives treatment now and that future management be planned carefully. This cannot be adequately undertaken in a prison setting, and is most appropriately arranged in a setting of a psychiatric unit near the patient's home, where the staff may liaise closely with workers in the community who will be responsible for the care of the family later. I am willing to offer your client and the Court any facilities at my disposal.

(Psychiatric report, case 4, female convicted of
causing grievous bodily harm)

From an impersonal perspective, this report and its recommendations are really quite remarkable. Here is a subject who for more than a year has been officially regarded as likely to commit homicide. The officials involved in the case have decided that she should none the less remain in the most intimate proximity to her anticipated victim, and they have knowingly arranged for her to spend many hours each day alone with this completely helpless child. She then fulfils the expectation, by attempting to stab the child to death. The original assessment of risk has now been proved manifestly correct, whilst the regime of treatment, support and surveillance has equally manifestly failed. The general prognosis has if anything deteriorated, and it is suggested that the risk to the victim will continue for several years. None the less, the officials concerned still insist that the desirable course of action is to reinstate the existing pattern of management, and as soon as possible to restore the offender to her original position of responsibility for her victim's safety and wellbeing. This is regarded as the ideal situation for all concerned.

Although all the uncomfortable facts are present in the report, the coherence of its recommendations are nowhere founded on any construction of the woman as either a violent and continuingly dangerous criminal, or a seriously ill subject for whom brief hospitalizations and community treatment have manifestly and devastatingly failed. What grounds the report is the apparently blinding construction of its subject *as a woman, as a mother, and as a wife*. Home and family are her proper place. Caring for her husband and children are her rightful activities. Tenderness towards her child is her natural emotion. The technical possibility of disrupting this domestic idyll by the preventive detention of the woman is dismissed in half a sentence. The report neither anticipates nor encounters any judicial opposition: the woman is ordered to her local hospital, with no restriction on her discharge.

Treatability and the amenable patient

This assumed harmlessness of the disordered female offender is one of the factors that improves her chances of being judged suitable for community-based treatment. Another factor is the perceived benefit of such treatment for women. Secure and custodial treatments tend to be seen as not only less likely to *help* disordered women, but also as more likely to *harm* them, by taking them away from their families, and robbing them of the kinds of sensitive interpersonal contact that are assumed to be vital for their mental health. Conversely, women are regarded as particularly susceptible to the kinds of psychiatric treatment that can be offered in the community, either through a psychiatric probation order or an unrestricted hospital order. What this means is that whilst a hard core of seriously disordered male offenders tend to be competing for a small share in the scanty resource of long-term provisions, female offenders (seriously disordered or otherwise) are seen as candidates for those forms of psychiatric provision that are most easily and widely available.

Needing comfort and support

Many of the female offenders dealt with through psychiatric treatment 'in the community' are diagnosed as suffering from some minor or chronic psychiatric condition. The provisions for psychiatric probation orders make even this degree of labelling unnecessary, however, and what is equally often provided in recommendations for such treatment is merely a descriptive indication of the offender's troubles, and the assertion that a doctor might be able to help:

> She would appear to have a confused sexual orientation and at the moment she has more of homosexual inclinations. I feel that she has various sexual conflicts, eating problems and poor control of her feelings (associated with menstruation). She would no doubt benefit by psychiatric treatment and I would be pleased to undertake her care as an out-patient.
>
> (Psychiatric report, case 50, female convicted of wounding)

'Very often in these cases [shoplifting or child abuse] I send a woman for reports. It's not because she's mentally ill *as such*. She may have very good reason to be stealing or bashing her children. [...] But I do think often they do have complicated problems, emotional problems, that sort of thing, and it may be that the doctor is going to be able to get through to them better and give them the help that they need.'

(Magistrate)

Various kinds of help can be offered through out-patient treatment, but a central component is often the assumed provision of a special *relationship* between the troubled offender and psychiatric personnel, through which her problems are to be relieved or resolved. In a very general way, this expectation owes something to the psychoanalytic approach to the treatment of offenders that I discussed in Chapter 4, although in the vast majority of cases the level of psychiatric engagement that is entailed here is a far cry from that of the psychoanalytic approach. The contact between the patient and the psychiatrist is commonly restricted to a brief appointment, once a month or less. The approach is generally a mixture of 'counselling', 'support', enquiries as to the patient's progress or 'coping' (since an important objective is the early detection of potential 'crises'), and the prescription of minor tranquillizers or anti-depressants. The goals of this work are modest and never amount to any such major reconstruction of the subject as might be undertaken in intensive psychotherapy. What the approach *does* share with the psychoanalytic approach, however, is its emphasis upon *speaking*.

Language and interiority

'A lot of the kind of men we get, the young lads, they're not accessible to that kind of help; strong silent type. You know? We can do valuable work with that sort, but it's more a practical kind. You know, we try to help them about getting a job, activities, housing. It can be very rewarding, but it's more at a practical level. To use a counselling approach they have to be more articulate ... able to talk about, to *verbalize* their problems. I think women are often better at that. I mean, we women are used to talking *to each other*, aren't we. But the best way to establish a rapport with a lot of the young lads is to do something practical. These days we're much more aware of the importance of practical projects for offenders, because it's not all of them that can use the counselling approach'.

(Probation officer)

Male offenders, in line with the pattern repeatedly noted, are presented as moving in a world of pure exteriority and action. Talking about feelings, experiences and inner problems is regarded as foreign, irrelevant or simply unhelpful to them. Yet for women offenders, such talk seems to offer the natural and necessary approach to that inner world from which their problems are assumed to arise. This is a world of which they *can* speak, being articulate and introspective creatures, but it is also a world of which they *must* speak, if they are to become sane, healthy and law abiding. Often even the crime itself is constituted as no more than a strangled utterance of this inner domain:

> She is currently unable to cope with these conflicts. Her offence was a way of telling us this.
>
> (Psychiatric report, case 38, female convicted of arson)

> A deterioration in the marital relationship ... culminated in the assault on [her child]. The wounding appears to have arisen ... as an attention-seeking act directed at her husband.
>
> (Psychiatric report, case 24, female convicted of manslaughter)

Where the crime is thus constituted as a pathological communication, the objective of treatment must be the establishment or re-establishment of a healthy and wholesome communication. It is words that give access to this troubled interior of women's feelings, and it is through the circulation of words that this space is to be regulated and kept under surveillance. It is assumed that for healthy and conforming women, marriage and the family will provide the natural locus of such communication. Often a central object of the therapeutic intervention is therefore the attachment or reattachment of the offender to a domestic group, within which this regulatory and health giving exchange of words can occur:

> She tells me she has never felt particularly close to her parents but realizes now how much they care about her ... recently she has begun to reveal to them all the anxieties which she previously kept to herself. She realizes that whatever the future may bring, she has to put much more effort into her relationships with other people, instead of keeping her thoughts and feelings to herself. She expresses motivation to change, but acknowledges it will not be easy to adjust her personality .... She does not appear to be suffering from any mental illness, but I understand that it is felt that she could benefit from out-patient treatment. It could be said that her offence was committed out of desperation to seek attention.
>
> (Social Enquiry Report, case 50, female convicted of wounding)

The woman who turns to crime is presumed to lack the crucial experiences of healthy communication. Psychiatric contact is expected to remedy this lack, by enabling her, albeit with difficulty, to develop the crucial faculties of insight and self-expression, and in the meantime to provide a surrogate field of communication, with which to compensate for the failures and inadequacies of her existing relationships. The appropriateness of this surrogacy is often inescapably predicated on the conception of the female offender as a perpetual *child*.

Subjects-in-the-process-of-becoming

As I mentioned before, little patience is offered to the 'childish' male offender. His irresponsibility is taken as a perverse and culpable state, which is simultaneously regarded as his own responsibility and as likely to be irremediable. It is this that underlies the perception of personality disorder and psychopathy as essentially untreatable in male cases. In my own sample, the only two exceptions to this involved males who were also diagnosed as mentally retarded.[19] Like many female offenders, these two subnormal men were seen as likely to benefit from continuing opportunities to grow up – though even so they were regarded as needing the security of a long-term custodial setting. The assertion of the 'childishness' of female offenders is intended to be sympathetic. It is taken to imply a genuine incompleteness of development, which gives grounds for therapeutic optimism. Right through adulthood, the female offender can still be treated as a subject-in-the-process-of-becoming; her refusal to conform and her failures to 'settle down', (often explicitly pathologized as 'personality disorders'), are assimilated to some obscure retardation of development, which a therapeutic relationship might remedy:

> She does require continuing psychiatric treatment which offers her the only prospect of a development and maturation of her personality. She is unlikely to receive treatment for her personality disorder if she remains in custody, and the circumstances of confinement are likely to be damaging .... I believe treatment could be undertaken if the defendant was to be made the subject of a probation order with a condition of psychiatric treatment.
> (Psychiatric report, case 24, female convicted of manslaughter)

Where the subject is conceived in these terms of incompleteness and neediness, the depiction of her offences as 'attention seeking' is not a pejorative matter, as it generally is in male cases. Like a child, the female offender is conceived as having genuine needs for attention, and as with a child, her cry for help becomes a legitimate communication, which should neither be ignored nor blamed. If the subject has had to turn to criminal behaviour then this is only a sign that the world has failed her, and that a closer, more understanding or more embracing support must be provided. The following case vividly exemplifies this reasoning. It is the case of a woman aged thirty-two, who has thirty-six previous convictions for a variety of acquisitive, violent and sexual offences, and who has been under intermittent psychiatric care since early adulthood. The diagnosis has usually been personality disorder, though this has been amended to psychopathy on each of the occasions when compulsory admissions have been imposed. She is now convicted of setting fire to a hotel where she had been refused the use of the telephone:

> It must be remembered that at the time of the firesetting, Miss Zimmerman was receiving almost the maximum amount of community support. She had a probation officer. She had an open appointment for a psychiatric clinic and she actually had a friend with her in the hotel when the fire was started. The only obvious addition might have been for her to have been a day patient in a psychiatric hospital; this might be tried in a future rehabilitation plan.

Talking to Miss Zimmerman and reading the rather pathetic and depressed letter which she wrote a few months before the firesetting, one can see the turn that events were taking. Miss Zimmerman has several difficulties with which to contend. Not only is she of dull intelligence, but she is also handicapped by institutionalization so that for her to make ordinary decisions is hard. While she needs structure in her life, she cannot for very long put up with ordinary rules in hostels. Without structure she immediately feels lonely and unsupported, and tends to drink heavily and contemplates or takes overdoses.

When she set fire in the Hotel, I doubt if she had any conscious intention of endangering the lives of other residents. I think she was feeling depressed and hopeless, and set the fire mainly to call attention to how she was feeling ....

There is little to be expected from specifically anti-depressant medication. Her depressive feelings are caused mostly by a situational reaction to ordinary life demands upon a person handicapped in both intelligence and personality. Only very gradual improvements are to be expected, and rehabilitation is likely to be a lengthy process ....

As far as I can judge the case as a psychiatrist, some residential placement is now necessary ...[but] of course the residential placement is not the end of the story. One must start again helping her to manage in the community once she is released and be endlessly patient to stand by her if further convictions occur in the future. When she is in the community again, I should be pleased to offer her psychiatric help as an out-patient.

(Psychiatric report, case 33, female convicted of arson)

The report recommends, and the court accepts, that the woman be made subject to a compulsory hospital order. The appropriateness of this disposal is constructed around a disparate assortment of arguments about the nature of the offence and the offender, all of which are characteristic of female cases, and none of which would commonly be invoked in the construction of a male case. These arguments progress in two different directions: on one side there are those that neutralize any contrary demands for a retributive disposal; on the other, more positively, there are those that stress the suitability of a medical one. Together the arguments of this passage will provide a concluding and summary illustration of all the dynamics discussed in this chapter.

First she can properly be relieved of moral responsibility for the crime itself. Instead of being seen as primarily a dangerous criminal act, the firesetting is merely part of 'the turn events were taking'; if it was an act at all, it was one performed without 'any conscious intention' of the danger. The offence is thus displaced from the moral calculation; there is nothing for which retribution need be demanded.

Second, any demands for punishment that may survive this displacement, are to be offset by the fact that this offender is already an unfortunate victim, already penalized by an undue burden of troubles. Her incompetence, her inability to 'put up with ordinary rules', her difficulty in making 'ordinary decisions', and the effects of previous institutional admissions, (even though these resulted from her own misbehaviours), are all constituted as afflictions for which she has no responsibility, and for which she therefore deserves compensation and sympathy rather than blame.

Thirdly she is also a *sick* subject: her low intelligence and unfortunate personality are here constituted as 'disorders', rendering her prone to the complications of depression, alcoholism and overdoses – not to mention criminal offending. This construction of her condition paves the way for the medicalization of her case as a whole.

Thus, fourthly, regardless of the tenuousness of any medical diagnosis and the absence of any specific medical treatment for it, this is still constituted as an appropriate case for medical intervention. There may be problems of providing sufficient community support to meet the requirements of a woman with tendencies towards dangerous misconduct if not given round-the-clock surveillance and support. But still the case is not regarded as inherently unsuitable for community care: the out-patient appointment and the psychiatric day hospital may still, in time, offer hope.

Fifthly and finally, this requirement of long-term, intensive support is constituted as a genuine and legitimate *need* of the subject. The woman's crime is a 'cry for help' in response to her experience of feeling 'lonely and unsupported'. Like a child she is entitled to receive that help, however insatiable the need and however long sustained. The remarkable but ultimately consistent conclusion of the report is thus a kind of blank cheque of therapeutic commitment; it appears as an unqualified promise of psychiatric credit to offset any future demands that she should pay for the offences of which she seems more victim than perpetrator. Here we have a final statement on all the female offenders discussed in this book. Here too we have a general watchword for all the professional agents, as they tortuously make sense of the behaviour of these women, and commit themselves to the only course of action that their construction then allows: *One must start again helping her to manage in the community ... and be endlessly patient to stand by her if further convictions occur in the future.*

Notes

1 e.g. *Kiely, AC, 20.12.66* quoted in Thomas (1979 p. 26); See also *Harvey & Ryan, 1971, Crim LR 664*, (transcript quoted in Walker and McCabe, 1973, p. 88).
2 This woman, (case 22), was eventually acquitted altogether: the jury came to the conclusion that she lacked even the degree of criminal intent for the crime of manslaughter.
3 i.e. Compulsory Hospital Order under the 1959 legislation; equivalent to a s 37 order under the 1983 Act.
4 See Parsons (1951 esp. Chapter 10) and Parsons (1950). The extention of such exemptions to antisocial behaviour is criticized in 'medicalization of social control' theories, e.g. Conrad and Schneider (1980).
5 See Foucault (1967); Scull (1979); Jones (1972).

6 See, for example, *Ashdown, 1974, Crim L Rev, 130*, upholding a sentence of life imprisonment on an 'untreatable' psychopath. See also Hines (1982, Chapter 11, part 5 and Chapter 12 part 1).

7 Six out of the eight male treatment orders were for in-patient treatment, and all but one of these included a restriction order. Of the seventeen female treatment orders, ten were for in-patient treatment, but only three included a restriction order.

8 My sample included more in-patient orders and fewer psychiatric probation orders than appear in the overall statistics. This is largely due to the biasing of my sample towards homicide cases.

9 See for example, reports in *The Times* on the cases of Horan (24.4.74); and Harding (15.6.83).

10 Thus even if one looks at cases with similar medical or criminal histories, the same male/female disparities remain. Illustrations of the almost perverse refusal to construe female offenders as dangerous enough to justify detention are given in both this and the following section.

11 Case 89.

12 See Floud and Young (1981) for an authoritative discussion of this area. See also the Butler Report (1975) and the May Report (1979), both of which reflect a growing concern over the risks posed to the public by mentally abnormal offenders.

13 e.g. Case 80.

14 See cases quoted at note 9, supra.

15 See Criminal Statistics. In 1985, for example, 58 per cent of female manslaughter and infanticide cases were dealt with by means of probation orders or non-restricted hospital orders, as compared to 8 per cent of the male cases.

16 Case 55.

17 See Kruttschnitt (1982, p. 495f); Eaton (1983).

18 This was the only category of offence which professional personnel regularly cited to me as one where the importance of psychiatric factors would be assumed in advance. In more academic circles, however, the 'disease model' of child abuse is currently receiving less favour. (See Parton, 1985, Chapter 6).

19 Cases 96 and 104.

Chapter seven:

In conclusion

The evidence given by psychiatric experts in criminal courts has three qualities.
  (a) It has, or may have, the power of life and death.
  (b) It functions as a discourse of truth, being scientific – it is given by people
      qualified within scientific institutions.
  (c) When one reads the transcripts, they make one laugh.
Such testimonies are an integral part of the daily juridical discourse.

(Foucault, 1975)[1]

As I outlined at the beginning, there is nothing immediately surprising about the disproportionate psychiatrization of women offenders. Psychiatric diagnosis is commoner for women than for men right across the population, and it is easy to assume that the disproportionate psychiatrization of female offenders must be merely the registration, within this particular setting, of a general epidemiological difference. Alternatively, the adoption of a psychiatric approach towards offenders is often presented as a form of judicial 'leniency' – and the notion that criminal courts are prejudicially lenient to female offenders is hardly a novel one. Without disputing the force of these observations, I have tried to stand back from the assumptions on which they are based, and to examine the sexual disparity of psychiatric sentencing as an issue in its own right. Instead of immediately demanding *why* this discrepancy should arise, and trying to relate the question to some overarching but remote parameter of sexual division or sexual difference, I have been asking precisely *how* it arises, in its own distinct social context and as a product of the specific processes of medical and legal decision making. This approach has enabled me both to dispute these initial assumptions and to suggest an alternative understanding.

My analysis has been at the level of the *discourses* of medicine and criminal justice. These discourses are not simply mystifying or irrelevant surfaces of *words*. On the contrary, they are ways of understanding, deciding and *doing* things; they are themselves the machinery of power in which both professionals and their subjects are equally enmeshed. In the decisions that I examine, it is the offenders who are most obviously coerced by the power of these discourses: it is on the course of *their* lives that these medico-legal pronouncements have the most poignant or violent impact. Yet the pronouncements of professional personnel are also constrained by the same power. Doctors and sentencers cannot make just *any* decision; in any particular case they cannot necessarily even make what they perceive to be the *best* decision. They too are constrained in their social actions by the discourses that they speak but cannot own.

Through my analysis I have sought to untangle the complex of factors within medical and legal discourse that systematically lead towards this sexually differentiated pattern of disposal. I have attempted to expose the theoretical assumptions and practical conditions through which these outcomes can become predictable and intelligible. In summary of this analysis the discrepancy can be related to the interaction of two internal 'structures' of these discourses, two sets of relatively stable conditions which organize and regulate the statements of medicine and the law, and constrain what decisions and judgments they can make. Each of these two structures separately conditions the final pattern of psychiatric sentencing, and together they provide the conditions for the sexual disparity.

The first of these structures regulates the practical involvement of psychiatry in criminal justice. It comprises a complex of formal and institutional provisions, spanning both medical and legal discourse. The most important of its many components are the legal statutes and guidelines governing the involvement of psychiatry in criminal justice, and the complex of medical facilities which may be made available for the treatment of offenders.

On its own, there is nothing in this structure of formal provisions that will adequately account for the sexual discrepancy. Certainly one can identify a few localized points where it would seem to favour the psychiatric disposal of female offenders, such as the special provisions for infanticide. But there are also elements within the whole that would seem, all things being equal, to work in the opposite direction. For example, compulsory hospital orders can only be made in cases involving imprisonable offences (a criterion that excludes a larger proportion of female than male offenders), whilst for female offenders there is more emphasis on psychiatric provision *within* the prison system, which might seem to offset the need for specifically medical disposals even amongst imprisonable offenders.

The second discursive structure is the set of premises and expectations that are invoked in assessing and judging the offender. These involve particular models of subjectivity, mentality and human nature, (formally explicated or otherwise) that inevitably influence the interpretation of the offender's behaviour, circumstances, biography, needs and deserts. Some of these assumptions are formally codified in legal statutes, doctrines and pronouncements. The doctrine of legal responsibility, for example, includes certain codified assumptions and presumptions about the nature and dynamics of criminal action. And the 'reasonable man test' embodies some formal instructions on how inferences are to be drawn as to the nature and reasonableness of human intentions. Other understanding about human subjectivity, (sometimes at odds with the legal ones), also appear in the formal theories and frameworks of psychiatric discourse, and determine what clinical diagnoses and labels can be attached to particular subjects.

These professional codifications are themselves embedded in a much wider and less regulated field of social understandings, belonging to the ordinary commonsense and everyday attitudes of the various agents concerned. In one sense these are extraneous and sometimes actually contradictory to the formal expectations of law or psychiatry, but they still provide a necessary resource upon which legal and medical reasoning inevitably and necessarily draws. Together, this accumulation of professional and of commonsense understandings establishes the broad discursive structure within which medical and legal agents make sense of the men and women who stand before them.

Across this broad discursive structure – unlike the other – the division by gender is both insistent and pervasive. As I have demonstrated, medico-legal discourse constructs male and female subjects in divergent terms. It cannot conceive of a subject in whom gender is not a fundamentally determining attribute, and at all levels the gender of the subject will influence the interpretation of behaviours and the assessment of appropriate responses. Thus materially similar events acquire different significances in the lives of male and female subjects; similar patterns of behaviour are differently interpreted as evidence of male or female personalities; and in male and female cases different criteria are called into play in assessing the 'same' parameters of legal culpability, personal pathology, and clinical need.

Yet although this discursive structure is clearly differentiated by gender, on its own it is no more able to account for the sexual disparity in disposal than is the structure of formal provisions. As before, it is possible to find some aspects of it that would seem, in an intuitive way, to predispose towards the psychiatrization of women. Some of the ways in which female behaviour is discussed, for example, seem to present the female subject in fundamentally pathological terms, as naturally irrational, unstable and out of control. But there are equally aspects of these gendered understandings which would appear, at this 'intuitive' level, to move in the other direction. Judicial personnel, for example, tend to regard male offenders as more likely than female to be 'really mad', and in male cases are more ready to interpret unruly or emotional behaviour as evidence of real mental pathology.

I am not therefore concluding that the discrepancy in the final distribution of disposals can be attributed either to direct sexual biases in the medical and legal provisions for them, or to any simple or systematic intention, whether in criminal justice or psychiatry, to psychiatrize female offenders *per se*. Although such biases *can* be traced at certain points in each of these structures, both fields are too rich in counter-examples, apparently favouring the psychiatrization of men, for these individual biases to be presented as a sufficient basis for the eventual unbalance.

At the analytic level, the central conclusion of this study is that the observable sexual discrepancy becomes both intelligible and predictable when viewed in the context of the *intersection and interaction* of these two broad structures. This perspective not only takes into account the more obvious points where female offenders tend to be pathologized and psychiatrized, but also has a rather more surprising effect: it shows how even those aspects of these discourses that seem, in isolation, to move in the *opposite* direction can in fact make a positive contribution to the final discrepancy.

Thus, for example, the typical construction of disorderly female offenders as if anything rather *less* deranged than disorderly males seems intuitively to militate *against* their psychiatric disposal. Against the particular background of existing legal and psychiatric provisions, however, this difference tends in fact to operate in *favour* of a psychiatric approach. On the legal side, the statutory provisions allow offenders to be given a psychiatric probation order whether or not any disorder is diagnosed, so within that particular framework of legal provisions, the perceived lack of specific disorder does not bar these women from psychiatric disposal. And on the medical side, the fashionable preference for consensual and community-based treatment actually makes it easier to offer medical treatment to those offenders who seem *least* disturbed and *least* in need of intensive medical supervision. Conversely, disordered male offenders tend to be perceived as very mad indeed, which might seem intuitively to suggest that they would be the favoured candidates for psychiatric disposal. But two other factors intervene: first the greater weight attached to moral and retributive factors in male cases, and second the grave shortage of facilities for the chronically or dangerously deranged. The interaction of these factors is unfortunate for the disordered male offender. In those relatively few cases where a male offender is so mad that the demands for retribution are in principle outweighed, he will often be seen as *too* mad to be treated in any of the conveniently available psychiatric facilities.

Although arguing that the relationship between gender and psychiatric sentencing is 'socially determined' and systematically produced through the operation of medical and legal discourse, I also maintain that this relationship is generally indirect, mediated, and removed from any specific or separately analysable tendency to psychiatrize criminal women 'in principle'. It may be the case that 'being a woman' a female offender is more likely than a male to be construed as meeting the theoretical and practical criteria which must be fulfilled before a psychiatric disposal can be made. But in the proper working of medicine and the law, it is never simply *because* the offender is a woman that a psychiatric disposal is preferred. The distinction is a delicate one, but none the less important. Analytically, it allows a more complete and consistent understanding of the empirical material; theoretically, it frees the explanation from the need to fall back on any abstract or ineluctable dynamic of sexual division; materially, it implies that quite predictable alterations in the current pattern of disposals could arise from changes in either of these two discursive structures, even if the other remained stable.

And a consideration of the conditions for change is entirely in order here. For I am aware that in revealing the 'intelligibility' of these decisions, (in their own internal terms and their own specific context), I have also, (from the commonsense perspectives of lay assessments), sometimes presented them as absurd. Some of the cases I have described have been bizarre, painful, and shocking, even in their initial constellations of material 'facts'. And in some of these, the subsequent deliberations of medicine and the law have led to judgments which in commonsense terms seem only to compound this initial bizarreness. I have, for example, revealed the 'intelligibility' of a system where a woman constituted as sane, who poured paraffin over her lodger and set fire to him, (as a response to his refusal to eat his supper), could be construed as a pitiable and helpless victim who should immediately be released as a subject deserving only compassion and support. And I have described how under the same system a suicidal and chronically disordered male, who poured paraffin over *himself* and set light to it, is treated as merely an 'angry inadequate arsonist', who should be punished as a criminal and refused all props of social or medical help. There are plenty more examples. My personal unease at many of these cases is irrelevant to my analysis, but will doubtless still have been evident in parts of my discussion.

Psychiatric and legal discourses are both, inevitably, sometimes remote from the commonsense world of lay assessments. And when they *interact* with each other, their divergence from the everyday reasoning of ordinary people is progressively amplified, so that the decisions that result (even if inexorably coherent in their own terms) are sometimes quite inexplicable to the lay observer. Even those who must speak these decisions are sometimes made uncomfortable by them. For the medical and legal personnel are themselves also commonsense subjects, caught up in the ordinary attitudes of everyday life. Often as these medical and legal personnel talked to me about their work, and described to me the recommendations and decisions that they had to make, there would come a moment when they suddenly acknowledged the conflicts between everyday reasoning and the constraints or contingencies of their work. A momentary pause, a wry smile, a shrug, or a shake of the head, and they would ask, 'But what else can we do?' And they would tell me then, (as if the object of my investigation were to reproach them, and some defence was therefore necessary), about the near impossibility of finding hospital beds for dangerous patients, about the real harm that was done to families by the imprisonment of mothers, about the self-destructive recalcitrance of recidivists who 'wouldn't learn', or about the regrettable failures of psychiatry to find practical remedies for psychopathy, social inadequacy, or simple human wickedness. 'It's the system', they would tell me, after a while. 'It's how things are. We do the best we can.'

So what might usefully be changed in this 'system' of medical and legal decision making? How could we relieve the contradictory pressures that beset the agents of these decisions, and that lead to such curious imbalances, (sexual and otherwise), in the final pattern of disposals? At the most fundamental level, what is actually required is clearly a complete reconstruction of the field: mere tinkering about with it is unlikely to do more than compound the existing mess. A consideration of the historical material shows that the current conglomeration of legal and medical provisions for the psychiatric treatment of offenders is hardly worthy of the title 'system'.

As I described, succesive generations of legal and medical innovators have defined particular groups of offender as posing medico-legal 'problems', and in a variety of well-intentioned but extemporary ways have attempted to make arrangements for the solution of these problems. Yet at each stage, these were different problems, conceived in different terms, leading to different types of remedy. The resulting hotch-potch of provisions was never 'developed', it simply 'accumulated'. And in consequence, our current decision-makers now lack any integrated system of provisions by which to plan and organize this aspect of their work. They are left to build solutions to modern problems out of the debris of historical failures. They are expected to justify their decisions through the rhetoric of long-dead strategies. There is obviously a need for a systematic review of the whole relationship between psychiatry and the law; for the development of a systematic strategy for any continuing psychiatric involvement with offenders; and for the construction, virtually from scratch, of an integrated body of legal provisions for those offenders whose mental condition calls for special treatment.

This reconstruction would present a major challenge for any government. Much of this study has been concerned with the detailed analysis of the many criteria that can influence the medico-legal calculations relating to each of the various psychiatric disposals that are currently available. The generality of many of these criteria may give some idea of the level of debate that would necessarily be involved in any attempt at reconstruction: it would be impossible to approach the task without confronting such major conceptual issues as the meaning of justice, the objectives of social control, and the nature of human subjects. Equally, the complexity of my discussion may give some indication of the multiplicity and intricacy of the questions that would have to be answered in order to establish new provisions. On what grounds, to what end and by whose authority should psychiatry involve itself in the treatment of offenders? What medical facilities or legal exemptions should be available, and to what kinds of offenders? What forms would such treatment take, and would it be offered or enforced? Who decides? Who knows? Who pays? I cannot answer these questions here. It has never been the objective of this study to construct any general programme of reform. What this study does allow, however, is a clarification of the kind of interventions that would effectively modify the specific sexual imbalances that I initially identified.

I have argued that the pattern of sexual discrepancy is a product of the interaction of a structure of medico-legal provisions and a structure of gendered understandings about the nature of human beings. Since it is an *interaction* that is involved, it follows that modifications in either of these structures would have an effect upon the pattern of sexual discrepancy. Changes could therefore be of two kinds.

In relation to the structure of legislative and institutional provisions, any of a large number of quite generally desirable reforms could have the simultaneous effect of reducing or modifying the sexual disparities. As an illustration, many of the most bizarre of my quotations from female cases are drawn from discussions of their 'criminal responsibility'. What sustains these discussions, and gives meaning to some of their most stilted statements about the mental contents of female subjects, is a conception of subjectivity that bears little relationship to contemporary understandings. Lord Devlin asserted that the terms in which the legal categories of responsibility, diminished responsibility, insanity and so on are defined are 'astringently logical'.[2] But if so, it is a logic which can lead to conclusions that seem nonsensical to ordinary reasoning, which ignore modern understandings of motivation, and which might well be challenged in a modern review of the mental component of crime. Even without modifying the curious conception of femininity which now enter the medico-legal assessment, the replacement of the archaically rationalistic conception of legal subjectivity with one that also gave attention to emotional forces and pathologies, might well allow female offenders to appear more 'normal' to the law, and might free official agents from drawing such oddly contradictory conclusions about the normality/pathology of their minds.

At the same time, any general 'tidying up' of the doctrines of legal responsibility might rethink the whole basis of the provisions for 'diminished' responsibility – an area where the sexual disparity is particularly marked. The restriction of this defence to cases of homicide is a direct reflection of the current mandatory sentence for murder. The practical need for it is further reinforced by the exclusion of convicted murderers from the provisions of the Mental Health Act. It is basically only this unique inability of the court to take psychiatric factors into account when *sentencing* convicted murderers that makes this special verdict either necessary or useful. If only judges were permitted the same discretion in the sentencing of murderers that they currently possess in relation to other categories of homicide, such as manslaughter, one might dispense with these special provisions altogether. In this way one could immediately erase the largest field of sexual differentiation in psychiatric verdicts, and pave the way for the treatment of all homicide cases to be decided at the same stage in the proceedings, and on the same terms. Alternatively, a rethinking of the general notion of criminal responsibility might expose advantages in retaining some notion of the partial disruption of criminal responsibility by reason of mental pathology – but if so, there seems no logical reason for restricting this to cases of murder.

Rather differently, but still in relation to decisions at verdict, this 'tidying up' of the existing provisions would almost certainly result in the timely abandonment of the unique and specifically sexualized criteria of infanticide. Although modern medical thought does admit the possibility of mental illness being precipitated by childbirth, these 'puerperal' disorders are no different in their symptoms from mental disorders that are precipitated in quite different ways. Against this context it hardly seems necessary for the law to invite such a specific pathologization of childbirth, let alone of lactation, which seem quite unassociated with mental disorder. And if there still seems a need for some special verdict that will make allowance for the more general stresses and distresses of family life, then it hardly seems necessary to exclude fathers, or siblings, or parents of older children, or those who commit other offences than homicide ... if one pushes the logic of the defence, one soon returns, almost unawares, to the need for a much more general framework for any special exemptions at verdict.

At the point of sentencing, there is doubtless even more to be done – not least because it is here that most psychiatric disposals are currently made. As I discussed in the latter chapters of this study, the current lack of any integrated system of medico-legal provisions is a crucial condition for the current disparities in the psychiatric treatment of convicted male and female offenders. The current situation offers the courts a variety of different and contradictory criteria on which to determine the appropriateness of a psychiatric disposal at the point of sentencing.

At present what tends to happen is that female offenders are assessed as appropriate for a psychiatric disposal in relation to one set of criteria, whilst males are assessed as inappropriate for such treatment by reference to quite different criteria. The Butler Committee, working in the early 1970s, merely endorsed this situation, which allows both courts and doctors, entirely at their own discretion, to prioritize clinical needs in relation to one case and to ignore them in the next.[3] A decade and a half since the Butler enquiry, it is surely now time for a new examination of the criteria both for the disposal of mentally abnormal offenders and for psychiatric involvement with offenders generally. The establishment of *any* consistent set of medico-legal criteria, to be applied in all cases, would almost certainly have the effect, *inter alia,* of reducing the sexual discrepancy. It might also, *inter alia,* necessitate a disturbing review of the current availability of psychiatric resources for offenders.

Perhaps the single most disturbing aspect of the current organization of this field is that there is no adequate strategy of provision for mentally abnormal offenders who might need long-term or secure psychiatric care. In the mid-1970s, following the urgent recommendations of the Glancy and Butler reports, central funds were allocated to the health authorities for the provision of secure custodial units, but health authorities are still being slow to establish these.[4] In any case the small number of places allowed for under this funding could not significantly dent the large backlog of demand, and in the foreseeable future it seems inevitable that large numbers of disordered but potentially dangerous offenders will continue to be sent to prison, as the only safe place to put them. The majority of these are male, but in individual terms the situation is equally shameful and unsatisfactory for that minority of extremely disturbed female prisoners, who are also barred from the treatment that they need.[5]

Members of the criminal justice professions are outraged at the position in which this shortfall of provision places them. Sentencers protest that 'putting people who are severely mentally ill into prison is a form of cruelty', and that the current situation, which obliges them to take responsibility for this cruelty, 'is intolerable'.[6] The Justices' Clerks' Society urged the inclusion within the new Mental Health Act of provisions whereby hospitals could be *compelled* to admit disordered offenders from the courts. No such steps were taken, and the society expressed its 'profound disappointment' at this failure by pointing out that 'it is nothing short of a public scandal that offenders who are mentally ill are being incarcerated in prisons at a time when the prison service is striving to cope with gross overcrowding in penal establishments'.[7]

The prisons do not, of course, enjoy any of the rights that hospitals have to select or reject their clientele; they have to take in, and somehow accommodate, whatever gets sent to them. How they do so, and the conditions under which inmates are housed and treated, is itself a matter of considerable concern.[8] Official Home Office figures minimize the number of mentally ill offenders who are sent to prison.[9] Independent research, however, invariably finds the prisons to be bursting with mentally disturbed inmates;[10] even the most conservative of studies finds rates of mental disorder that are many times higher than the figures provided by the prison service.[11] A handful of mentally disordered prisoners do eventually get transferred to hospitals after their sentences commence,[12] but as a Home Office study discovered,[13] even relatively sympathetic Health Service consultants are unwilling to accept prisoner-patients who may need long-term care or are violent. These mainstream psychiatrists still see their role as largely confined to short-term treatment and rehabilitation, and want nothing to do with prisoner-patients who can not fit in with these expectations.

In relation to this structure of formal provisions and facilities, the sexual discrepancy in psychiatric disposal must be seen more as a deficiency of psychiatry in relation to male offenders than as an excess in relation to females. Specifically, it is a deficiency in the kinds of provisions that male offenders are commonly assumed to require. From this perspective, the most obvious means of righting the disparity would be simply to shift the balance of medio-legal provision, so that more is made available to mentally disordered subjects who also seem dangerous, intractable and possibly rather wicked.

But there is another possibility. Rather than theorizing the imbalance as a failure to provide the psychiatric facilities that disordered males are presumed to need, one could relate it to the failure of psychiatry and criminal justice to see male offenders as suitable for the provisions that are currently available. The assumption of male intractability often makes them unwelcome to modern 'short-stay' psychiatric units. The expectation of male dangerousness often makes them seem unsuitable for treatment in open wards or on probation. The presumption of 'deliberate badness' often makes them seem underserving of the benefits of psychiatry. Even prior to any evidence, and often despite it, these prejudices direct the deliberations about male offenders away from psychiatric disposal, just as the opposite ones direct the assessment of female offenders towards it. In seeking to reduce the disparity in psychiatric disposals, it might therefore be equally pertinent to challenge this structure of medico-legal prejudice.

My own distaste for divisions of gender and my own disbelief in 'essential' moral or mental differences between male and female subjects are doubtless evident in this study. Accordingly I am committed to principles of fairness and formal equality, even if this means taking away from women some of the 'advantages' of gender that their femininity had brought them. And an uncomfortable conclusion of my study is that this could certainly be involved in any 'righting of the balance'. Contrary to my initial political prejudices, which saw the excess of psychiatry as personally oppressive to female offenders, it became increasingly clear as the analysis progressed that on the whole female offenders do rather well out of it. Rhetoric aside, it is difficult to suggest that the flimsy surveillance provided by an occasional out-patient appointment is more irksome or humiliating to the women concerned than the alternative penal sanctions, especially imprisonment. And my demand that men and women should be treated on the same terms could certainly be taken as implying that more of these women should be subjected to ordinary punishment. As a feminist this conclusion rather galls me, and aside from introducing some quite general critique of the existing penal system, I am not sure how my analysis would allow this implication to be countered or neutralized. But the essential principle remains: in the long term, and irrespective of the immediate advantages to particular individuals, the struggle for women's equality will never be furthered by the attempt to retain either the privileges or the disabilities of femininity.

In relation to the particular issues of psychiatric sentencing, however, my objections to such divisions are also motivated by more general concerns with issues of psychiatry and the law. Often the differentiated assumptions that are made about male and female offenders, without question or challenge, have seemed to cloud the whole assessment of their cases, and to lead to decisions that seem either unnecessarily inhumane to the offender or unnecessarily dangerous for the public. There are therefore practical and pragmatic reasons for seeking change, as well as theoretical and feminist ones.

So what changes do I have in mind? I am not suggesting that the division by gender can be simply expunged. I take for granted that a human subject with its sex eliminated is in practice as unthinkable to the ordinary agents of criminal justice, (or indeed to the ordinary subjects of their decisions), as it is to the Court of Appeal.[14] Yet even without proposing anything so radical, it may still be possible to query the *meanings* that are attributed to this division, and the oddness of the assumptions that get attached to it.

I suggest that the terms in which the sexual division is constructed in these medical and legal decisions produces versions of male and female reality that are neither necessary nor useful. They are not consistent with what we understand about the human condition when we think about it most clearly and carefully. They cannot even be assimilated to the banal and conventional wisdom of common sense. The feckless females with their reason in knots and all conscious intentionality erased; the cartoon males in whom even madness or suicide have no inner content .... Some of the characters whom I have lifted from these medical and legal texts must appear at least as amputated or improbable as that hapless 'human being with its gender eliminated'.

It is probably true that many of the constituent terms that enter these constructions are the grindingly familiar ones of everyday sexism: there is nothing unfamiliar for example in the notion of women as passive and emotional or of men as active and insensitive. Such notions doubtless deserve fighting in their own right, although that is another and more general struggle altogether. For the immediate point here is that the tactics whereby those initially familiar terms are woven together in the construction of medical and legal subjects are quite specific to these discourses: the gendered subjects presented in these texts are far stranger than the everyday stereotypes of ordinary sexism. Also specific are the particular syllogisms of reasoning which then appropriate these subjects and decide how they should be treated: some of the judgments that I have discussed in this text diverge radically from the expectations of even an averagely sexist onlooker. These curious constructions and judgments arise only in the *interweaving* of medical, legal, and everyday discourse; the particular form and consequences of these divisions are not reducible to any of these discourses on its own.

But in attempting to make sense of this structure of sexual divisions, one can trace in both the male and the female cases certain possibilities of understanding that have a positive value – even at the moment when their extreme polarization stretches commonsense understandings to the limit. In the male and female cases that I have described in this book, one can find two divergent ways of seeing, understanding and judging criminal subjects. Neither separately nor together can they claim any essential 'correctness', but together they might allow an understanding of human beings that is more intelligible and less debilitating than either of them on its own.

From the construction of male cases, we may learn that it is possible to confront even the most extreme or abnormal of human behaviours, without suspending the acknowledgment of a conscious human subject as the agent of that behaviour, without pathologizing him, and without obscuring the social meanings and consequences of his deeds, in the full reality of their harm and threat. And from the construction of female cases, we may learn that even the most destructive and unregulated of criminals – to say nothing of the hordes of more petty ones – may be judged in ways that do not exile them from human feelings or pity, that do not strip them of their alternative and less shameful social statuses, and that do not dismiss as irrelevant all the multiplicity of pressures and all the weight of reasons and of unreason that everywhere condition human actions. *Both* of these perspectives could be usefully and humanely applied to offenders of *either* sex.

To desire the wisdom of both perspectives and yet wish to detach them from the division by gender is not intended as either conciliatory or paradoxical. It may indeed be unthinkable for medicine or criminal science to treat their subjects as anything other than gendered men and women. But to accept that men are men and that their crimes can be dangerous and wicked need not blind us to what is painful and disordered in their experience, nor to the possibility that their inner troubles might warrant compassion or treatment. And to accept that women are women and that their inner lives are sometimes tragic or bewildering or constrained need not obscure the fact that women also have lives in the material world, and responsibilities for those lives that no amount of psychiatry can erase. Such an extension of perspectives might also allow a more equitable strategy of disposal – even though it cannot make the problems less insistent or the decisions any easier.

Notes

1 Michel Foucault, Lecture at the College de France, 'Les Anormaux', 8.1.75.
2 Devlin (1963, p. 85) quoted more fully in section on insanity, Chapter 2.
3 The report states that 'The theory behind the present practice ... has our full support'. It goes on to outline as this 'present practice' the courts' complete discretion in choosing between options of deterrent, preventive, reformatory, retributive and finally therapeutic approaches to disordered offenders.
4 See Higgins (1984).
5 See Carlen (1983, p. 195); See also Chapter 5 note 17, supra.
6 Appeal Court judgment in *Harding*, quoted in *The Times*, 15.6.83.
7 Justices' Clerks' Society, 1982, p. 5.
8 See Carlen (1986) in Miller & Rose, (eds) (1986).
9 See report of the Work of the Prison Service (1984); Cheedle and Ditchfield (1982).
10 Faulk (1976) for example, whose study included personality disorders amongst the conditions taken into account, found that the large *majority* of offenders in an ordinary male prison were mentally disordered.
11 See Coid (1984) for a review of this literature.
12 This is provided for under Mental Health Act 1983, 47.
13 Cheedle and Ditchfield (1982, Chapter 3).
14 See comments on *Camplin 2 All ER 168*, discussed in final sections of Chapter 2.

Appendix A

Official statistics on psychiatric disposals

The statistics quoted here are drawn from the annually published Criminal Statistics for England and Wales, (HMSO), with the exception of figures for psychiatric probation orders, 1950–1970, which are from unpublished Home Office Statistics for England and Wales, quoted in Walker and McCabe, (1973, p. 66) and findings for insanity and unfitness to plead for 1983, which are from the Prison Statistics for England and Wales (HMSO). All statistics relate to offenders aged twenty-one and over. The latest figures available in March 1987 were for 1985.

Notes to Table 1

1 Changes in legislative provision since 1950 result in certain inconsistencies in the categories of disposal appearing in this table.
(a) *Mental deficiency*: Until 1959, the Mental Deficiency Act 1913 permitted mentally defective imprisonable offenders to be compulsorily admitted to an 'appropriate institution'. These provisions were superseded by the provisions of the Mental Health Act 1959 (see Walker and McCabe, 1973, p. 59). There is some chronological overlap, due to delay in the operationalization of the 1959 Act, and the inclusion in later years of uncompleted cases awaiting decision under the earlier legislation.
(b) *'Unfit to plead'*: Prior to the Criminal Procedure (Insanity) Act 1964, those found unfit to plead appeared in the statistics as 'insane on arraignment'. Following the Butler Report in 1975, they are listed as 'under disability in relation to the trial'.
(c) *Insanity*: Offenders found to be insane were categorized as 'guilty but insane' prior to the 1964 Act, and as 'not guilty by reason of insanity' thereafter.
(d) *Diminished responsibility*: This was not available as a defence prior to the Homicide Act 1957.
(e) *Hospital orders* (restricted and unrestricted): these become available only with the Mental Health Act 1959.

Where particular disposals were not legally available in the year in question the relevant cells are blocked out (i.e. '———'). Where they were available but not used, they are recorded as '0'.

2 Figures for 'psychiatric probation orders' include all orders in which a condition of psychiatric treatment is imposed, whether or not a residential (in-patient) requirement is also included.

3 Adjusted Totals. The figures used in calculating the final rate of psychiatric disposals have been adjusted in order to compensate for those cases, from 1959 onwards, which are recorded as infanticide or diminished responsibility *and also* dealt with by means of a treatment order under the Mental Health Acts. Without these adjustments, these cases would be counted twice – once as a psychiatric disposal at point of verdict and once as a psychiatric order at sentence. It has unfortunately not been possible to make the same adjustments in relation to diminished responsibility and infanticide cases dealt with by means of psychiatric probation orders, since the published figures for psychiatric probation orders do not include detailed breakdowns by category of offence.

4 No figures are available for psychiatric probation orders, 1971–8. Figures have not been published for findings of insanity or unfitness to plead since 1983. Totals for these years in which complete figures are not available are recorded in brackets.

Table 1: Psychiatric disposals, 1950–1983, all offences, all courts, by sex and type of disposal*

	Unfit to plead		Insane		Infanticide		Diminished responsibility		Mental deficiency		Unrestricted hospital order		Restricted hospital order		Psychiatric probation**		Total		Adjusted total***	
	M	F	M	F	M	F	M	F	M	F	M	F	M	F	M	F	M	F	M	F
1950	33	14	28	4		26	—	—	206	48	—	—	—	—	577	130	844	222		
1951	29	12	12	4		16	—	—	82	7	—	—	—	—	661	136	784	177		
1952	31	12	17	2		19	—	—	72	4	—	—	—	—	595	140	715	173		
1953	41	7	26	3		18	—	—	73	5	—	—	—	—	597	152	737	185		
1954	40	7	29	7		19	—	—	123	35	—	—	—	—	616	146	808	214		
1955	35	9	20	10		13	—	—	125	7	—	—	—	—	656	154	836	193		
1956	37	12	28	3		12	—	—	39	3	—	—	—	—	702	137	806	167		
1957	40	12	16	1		16	8	3	59	7	—	—	—	—	718	137	841	176		
1958	43	7	12	1		10	22	3	26	12	—	—	—	—	655	127	758	160		
1959	49	13	23	2		14	18	0	27	0	—	—	—	—	738	143	855	172	855	171
1960	37	8	16	1		18	17	6	26	4	71	23	17	3	771	154	955	217	955	217
1961	41	7	7	3		14	24	12	—	—	609	123	135	15	625	114	1468	288	1459	280
1962	28	8	9	0		17	26	8	—	—	606	144	126	11	648	189	1443	377	1429	366
1963	25	5	3	0		14	40	8	—	—	736	173	143	11	771	170	1718	381	1699	371
1964	25	8	4	0		7	26	9	—	—	786	116	114	10	807	197	1762	347	1740	340
1965	27	4	3	0		12	35	8	—	—	727	122	107	14	891	193	1790	353	1770	343
1966	18	1	2	0		16	39	7	—	—	825	123	96	9	897	217	1877	373	1853	367

(*See Notes to Table 1 note 1; ** ibid. note 2; *** ibid. note 3)

(Table 1, continued: Psychiatric disposals, 1950–1983)

	Unfit to plead		Insane		Infanticide	Diminished responsibility		Mental deficiency		Unrestricted hospital order		Restricted hospital order		Psychiatric probation		Total		Adjusted total	
	M	F	M	F	F	M	F	M	F	M	F	M	F	M	F	M	F	M	F
1967	35	2	2	1	12	30	10	—	—	755	110	129	16	1104	243	2055	403	2032	397
1968	24	4	0	3	17	29	10	—	—	724	116	126	15	1120	263	2023	428	2003	421
1969	25	4	5	0	9	28	12	—	—	762	104	145	12	1096	214	2061	355	2041	343
1970	19	3	2	0	8	49	10	—	—	738	114	168	10	1078	226	2054	371	2028	366
1971	25	6	2	3	12	45	13	—	—	724	92	134	14	†no figures		(930)	(140)	(903)	(132)
1972	32	6	0	1	12	48	15	—	—	607	102	130	11	no figures		(817)	(140)	(788)	(132)
1973	27	8	6	1	12	52	15	—	—	647	112	154	15	no figures		(886)	(163)	(861)	(155)
1974	22	8	3	0	13	63	27	—	—	561	78	124	12	no figures		(773)	(138)	(749)	(132)
1975	20	6	6	1	5	46	17	—	—	678	113	106	20	no figures		(856)	(160)	(842)	(149)
1976	31	4	5	1	4	62	20	—	—	581	110	92	21	no figures		(771)	(160)	(750)	(153)
1977	21	3	1	1	2	56	17	—	—	544	83	60	9	no figures		(682)	(124)	(664)	(117)
1978	13	2	2	1	5	55	14	—	—	486	100	77	9	no figures		(689)	(131)	(671)	(126)
1979	17	2	1	0	8	72	20	—	—	405	109	62	14	781	231	1338	384	1322	376
1980	29	0	2	1	6	59	12	—	—	437	115	78	17	873	325	1478	476	1465	468
1981	20	5	3	0	7	67	20	—	—	439	140	77	15	736	231	1342	418	1313	405
1982	25	4	0	1	1	60	13	—	—	426	86	105	11	780	225	1396	341	1369	338
1983	11	2	1	0	5	59	14	—	—	322	103	75	13	833	182	1301	319	1277	312
1984	(figures not published)†		(figures not published)†		5	55	15	—	—	557	112	85	15	777	185	(1474)	(317)	(1448)	(307)
1985	(figures not published)		(figures not published)		2	46	14	—	—	357	117	76	14	750	161	(1409)	(308)	(1388)	(302)

† See notes to Table 1, note 4.

Appendix B

The sample of cases

Criteria and method of selection

The major body of material analysed in this study consists of a retrospective sample of 129 cases heard at three London Crown Courts, drawing on court records of completed cases. Three major considerations guided the choice of these cases.

First, there were simple and pragmatic considerations as to the size of the samples and the volume of material that could be analysed. I wished to gather a body of material large enough for qualitative comparisons to be made between cases of different kinds, and yet small enough for quite detailed analysis of the sample as a whole. I began this study by examining all the cases of homicide by women heard in a single court over a two-year period. This sample, (24 cases in all), seemed on initial analysis to provide a varied but manageable body of material. In selecting other samples of cases, relating to different offences, I therefore chose to keep sample size in this same general region.

Second, I was concerned to select a group of cases which would include a reasonable number of psychiatric disposals. Given that psychiatric disposals account for only one or two cases per thousand, an entirely random sample of cases would be likely to throw up at most one or two psychiatric disposals, and probably none whatsoever. Two ways of circumventing this problem seemed feasible. The first was to select cases purely by reference to disposal, first taking cases in which a psychiatric disposal was recorded, and then, for comparison, taking a more random group of cases in which other disposals were made. This approach would have allowed an easy control over the number of psychiatric disposals available for consideration, but it also had certain disadvantages.

For the third consideration was the wish to gather a body of material that would allow a detailed examination of the process of reasoning and negotiation by which particular cases came to be categorized as appropriate or inappropriate for psychiatric involvement. In this context it seemed desirable not only to consider those cases in which a psychiatric disposal was ultimately made, in comparison with others drawn randomly, (in the majority of which a psychiatric disposal would never have been considered), but also to examine cases in which a psychiatric approach was considered but rejected. These 'failed' psychiatric cases seemed likely to prove particularly revealing of the factors that were critical in deciding the 'successful' ones. A sample selected by ultimate disposal might well include borderline cases on the 'successful' side of the divide, but in view of the relatively small number of cases in which psychiatric factors are even raised, there was no reason to suppose that a random sample of other cases would be likely to include any borderline cases in which the decision swung the opposite way.

A second method of selection was adopted in order to avoid this problem. This was to select the samples randomly from those offence groups in which psychiatric disposals are commonest, and from which even a random selection of cases might be expected to draw a reasonable number of both psychiatric and other disposals, including cases which were marginal on either side. In relation to the field as a whole, such a sample produces a somewhat distorted distribution of outcomes, with a bias towards psychiatric disposals. It did, however, allow the whole gradation of cases, (from those in which psychiatric considerations were never introduced to those in which their centrality was never disputed), to be retained and examined.

A serendipitous effect of this method is that the groups of crime where psychiatric disposals are highest overall are also those where the male/female disparity is also the greatest. For example, whereas women defendants are about twice as likely overall to receive a psychiatric disposal, in cases of homicide they are four or five times as likely to receive such a disposal. It is therefore possible that these areas of sentencing may provide an extreme and exaggerated reflection of the processes through which the (generally less conspicuous) discrepancy is produced across the field as a whole. If this is the case, the very distortions of this reflection should allow the phenomena of interest to be more easily identified and examined.

It goes without saying that such an approach, with its deliberate utilization of atypical fields, in which the distribution of relevant phenomena is exaggerated and skewed away from the norm, precludes absolutely the drawing of quantitative conclusions about the field as a whole. It must be emphasized, if not already obvious, that the object of this survey was always qualitative rather than quantitative. In a sense, the relevant 'quantitative' statistic, (the overall discrepancy in sentencing which can be noted from the official statistics), is already established in advance of the analysis, as described in Chapter 1. (The relevant figures from the official statistics are also set out in Appendix A.) What was intended in my own analysis was some form of explanation of *how* this quantitative difference arises, and a question of this form can only be approached through a qualitative approach.

On this basis, the main bodies of cases examined were drawn from three groups of crime, all of which have a relatively high rate of psychiatric disposal: homicide, other violence against the person, and arson. A second reason for including homicide cases is that two of the special psychiatric disposals, (findings of diminished responsibility and infanticide), are *only* available in homicide cases.

One problem with this approach, (which may be noted in a cautionary sense, even though it is not resolved), is that it depends on an initial assumption that the factors which produce the sexual discrepancy are ultimately homogeneous across all cases. It assumes that differences in the degree of this discrepancy in different areas of crime arise only from a difference in the 'intensity' with which these factors operate, and not from any more fundamental difference in the kinds of consideration which are at issue. It is thus assumed, for example, that the factors which produce a relatively modest sexual discrepancy in relation to offences of forgery, are in effect a 'diluted' version of the factors that operate to produce a very much more marked discrepancy in cases of homicide or arson.

The only way in which this assumption was in any way tested was by the inclusion of a small sample of cases involving acquisitive offences, (theft, robbery and burglary), for which the rate of psychiatric sentencing of both male and female offenders approximates closely to the overall figure. As can be seen in Table 2, these cases evidenced much the same pattern of recommendations as the others, and in the course of the analysis, no differences were evident in the kinds of argument that were deployed. This would seem to reinforce the assumption of a general homogeneity in the factors concerned in producing the discrepancy, and certainly give no reason to reject this assumption. In the light of both the smallness of the samples and the deliberate selection of atypical groups of cases, however, all the usual caveats must be raised with regard to extrapolating from the findings of this study to the larger population.

On the basis of the considerations discussed above, the following samples of cases were finally selected:

1 All the female homicide cases that were heard over a two-year period in one Crown Court (24 cases in all).
2 A sample of male cases, matched to the first sample by offence group and drawn from the same court and the same period of time (25 cases in all).
3 An additional, (overlapping), sample of male cases, matched to the first sample by offence group and victim (11 additional cases: where possible, the female cases were matched using cases already collected in sample 2).
4 180 male cases and 100 female cases drawn from three Crown Courts, involving offences of the various types mentioned above, viz. arson, violence against the person, and acquisitive offences. After an initial examination of all these cases, the analysis was focused on those cases for which a psychiatric report was available (36 male and 33 female cases).

Information on each of the cases examined in detail (129 in all) is given in this Appendix, Table 2.

Cases were initially drawn from court lists. These lists are compiled on a daily basis, and include the name of each defendant whose case begins that day, the number of the court file relating to the case, and the offence charged. Cases were selected from this list by starting at an arbitrary date and working through the list, selecting out each of the female cases charged with the offence shown, until the chosen number of cases had been found. Male cases were then selected by starting at the same point in the list, and again selecting each relevant case, consecutively, until the same number of cases had been found.

Since these lists include the full names but not the sex of defendants, cases were selected on the basis of first names. I therefore discounted cases with ambiguous or unrecognized first names, in which the sex of the defendant was not clear from the information given. This inevitably had the effect of selecting out some of the cases with foreign names – a small proportion of the total.

Material in files

Court files are variable in their content. In some instances they contain very full details of the case, in others very little. In theory they should contain all the documents received by the court relating to the case, ranging from the correspondence between the court and solicitors concerning legal aid expenses, to copies of witness statements, police photographs, and notes passed between the jury and clerks of courts. In practice, however, many of the files were incomplete, and consequently some of the relevant information about some of the cases was missing.

The most important documents for the current analysis were the medical reports and those relating to the sentence. Full discussion of the content of medical reports and sentencing decisions is included in the body of the text, and summarized in Table 2. Additionally, the following documents were noted in each case, and used wherever relevant:

Case record sheets: These are brief documents of standard format, which provide basic information about the defendant, (name, address, date of birth, sex etc.); the charge or charges; the defendant's plea; and the brief details as to the course and conduct of the case, (where and when heard, by whom and with what outcome).

Case summaries: Summaries of cases (about 200–300 words long) are written up by the clerks prior to the trial. These include, usually, a bald statement of the alleged crime and its circumstances, and an indication of the defendant's likely plea.

Records of police interrogations: Following the arrest of a suspect and during the investigations, formal interrogations of the defendant by the police are 'contemporaneously recorded' – i.e. the questions and answers are written down in long-hand by a second police officer. Following the interview, the subject is required to confirm the correctness of the record by signing each page and initialling each entry.

Other police records: The police also provide details of any known criminal record of the defendant, brief 'social' details, including any information known or discovered by them as to the defendant's background, employment, schooling, financial circumstances etc.

Social enquiry reports: These are prepared by probation officers, or occasionally by other social workers. They are between one and five pages long, and normally include a description of the offender's biography, family, employment and living situation, along with reflections or information on the offender's personality (including any psychiatric problems), and on the offence. Often there is also an explicit or implicit recommendation as to sentence. If the defendant is pleading guilty, the probation report may be prepared pre-trial, but in most cases it is prepared between conviction and sentence. Social enquiry reports are routinely prepared in cases involving (a) the most serious offences; (b) women defendants where a prison sentence might be imposed; (c) any other case where it seems likely that social factors may be relevant to sentence.

Legal documents: Most important here are the advisory documents relating to any problematic or unusual legal issues arising in particular cases. Such written 'advice' generally consists of a detail exposition of the potential relevance of specific elements of the evidence to the lines of legal argument that might be raised. These documents also quite frequently include advice as to the likely benefit of seeking a psychiatric report.

Judicial pronouncements concerning the case: All trials are recorded in shorthand but these records are not routinely transcribed. In special cases, however, the judge may request that some particular passage of evidence or judgment be transcribed and retained in the file. This is occasionally done, for example, where the sentencer passes an unusual sentence, and wishes his or her reasons for so doing to be available in the event of the defendant reappearing before the same court.

Supplementary homicide cases: 'male domestic killings'

One of the most immediately striking differences between male and female homicide cases (both in my own sample and across the field as a whole) is in the pattern of victimization: the vast majority of female cases involve 'domestic' killings, in which the victim is a sexual partner (past or present), or a member of the defendant's family or household. Male homicides, on the other hand, tend to include a higher proportion of attacks on strangers, and more cases where the killing takes place in the context of some other crime, such as burglary or robbery. It seemed possible that this difference in victimization was an important factor in the different treatment of male and female killers. To test this possibility, an additional quota of male cases was selected, so as to allow a closer matching of male and female cases by reference to victim. In fact the substitution of this second, matched, sample made no significant differences to the findings. The same general differences in both the medico-legal deliberations and in the final pattern of disposal could be traced whether or not the cases were matched by victim. In the specific comparison of male and female homicide cases, in Chapter 3, the original sample of male cases was therefore used, since there seemed no gain in arbitrarily replacing a randomly selected group of cases with one that was deliberately atypical. Reports relating to these cases were, however, included in the general analysis of sentencing decisions, in Chapters 5 and 6, and details of them are included in Table 2, following. (Cases 86–96)

(Notes regarding the significance of the various columns and the abbreviations used are included at the end).

Table 2: Cases, diagnoses, and outcomes
(Notes regarding the significance of the various columns and the abbreivations used are included at the end).

FEMALE HOMICIDES

No.	Age	Charge (note 1)	Conviction (note 1)	Victim	Reports (note 2)	Diagnoses (+ other comments) (note 3)	Disposal (note 4)
1.	24	murder	Ms (DR NI)	girlfriend	PMO/NHSx2	*Pp* (lesbian/OD's/psy.hist')	6 years prison
2.	38	murder	Ms (DR)	girlfriend	SER/SHx2/PMO	*Pp/Dp* (lesbian/psy.hist')	life prison
3.	27	murder/arson	as charge	acquaint.	PMOx2/NHS	?*Pp* (lesbian/Dp/Low IQ/alcoholic)	life prison
4.	31	attempt.murder	GBH	own child	SER/NHS	*Dp.* (psy.hist'/emotionally flat)	hospital order s 60
5.	19	infanticide	as charge	newborn	SER/SW/NHS	(abnormal state/confused/shock)	probation + psych.
6.	25	murd./Msx2/ars.	as charge	lover's wife/child.	NHS/NHS/PMO	(stress/hysterical/confused)	life prison
7.	60	murder	Ms, (NI,P)	lodger	SER/NHS	(nervous/alcoholic/anxious)	2 years SSSO
8.	29	murder	Ms,(P)	boyfriend	PMO/SER	PD (isolated/repressed)	probation
9.	57	attempt.murder	GBH	ex-husband	GP/NHSx2/SER	*depression* (stress)	2 yrs SSSO
10.	35	murder	NG	husband	PMO/SER	(alcoholic/depressed)	(not guilty)
11.	48	murder	Ms(NI)	husband	PMO/SER	(alcoholic)	18mnths SSSO
12.	22	murder	Ms(NI)	boyfriend	SER/PMO	(distressed/grief reaction)	18mnths SSSO
13.	22	murder	Ms(P, NI)	father	NHS/SER	(shock/grief)	probation
14.	19	murder/cruelty	inf'cide	infant	NHSx2/SER	Dp (sexual/social/family probs)	psychiatric probation
15.	22	murder	Ms(NI)	employer's baby	NHS/SER	(lonely/immature/?premenstrual)	2 yrs SSSO
16.	33	murder	Ms(DR)	son (5yrs)	SER/NHS/PMO	*reactiveDp* (relationship probs)	hospital order, s 60
17.	18	inf'cide	as charge	infant	SER/NHS	(emotional and sexual probs)	probation order with informal treatment
18.	33	murder	unfit to plead	mother	PMO/NHS	*schizophrenia*	detained in special hospital

No.	Age	Charge	Victim	Plea	Reports	Diagnoses (+ other comments)	Disposal
19.	26	murder	daughter (14 mnths)	Ms(DR)	SER/NHSx2	*schizophrenia* (psy.hist')	hospital order ss 60, 65
20.	40	murder	husband	Ms(P)	NHS/SER	*reactive Dp* (grief/stress)	probation with informal treatment
21.	55	manslaughter	stranger	as charge	NHSx2/SER	*chronic schizophrenia*	2 yrs SSSO informal treatment
22.	22	murder	boyfriend	not guilty	SER/NHS	(mental anguish since killing)	not guilty (informal treatment arranged)
23.	30	murder	stranger	Ms(DR)	SER/PMO/SH	*PD* (low IQ/alcoholic/psy.hist')	life prison (reduced to 6 yrs on appeal)
24.	32	murder	daughter (aged 3)	Ms(DR)	SER/NHS/PMO	*PD/?Dp* (family probs/alcohol abuse)	psychiatric probation

FEMALE ARSON

No.	Age	Charge	Reports	Diagnoses (+other comments)	Disposal
25.	27	arson	NHS	*reactive depression* (psychiatric history)	psychiatric probation order
26.	65	arson	NHSx3/PMO/SER	*?schizophrenia* (trial will worsen health)	not to be proceeded with
27.	39	arson/burglary	SER/PMO	*personality ais.* (unstable mood/alcoholic/psy.hist')	2 years SSSO informal psychiatric treatment
28.	40	arson	NHSx2?/PMO	*chronic schizophrenia* (?can no longer cope at home)	hospital order, s 37
29.	29	arson	SER/PMO	(extreme loneliness/alcoholic/behaviour probs/low IQ)	psychiatric probation
30.	68	arson	SER/Private	(alcoholic/eccentric)	18 months SSSO
31.	37	arson	NHSx2/SER	(in therapy/disturbed/isolated/'cry-for-help')	psychiatric probation
32.	22	arson	NHSx2/Private	(low IQ/immature/deprived/can't cope/usually pleasant)	psychiatric probation therapeutic community
33.	32	arson	NHSx2/PMO/SER	*psychopath* (depressive/low IQ/problems/damaged)	hospital order ss 60, 65
34.	28	arson	SER/Priv/NHS	*psychopath* (suicidal/alcoholic/self-harm)	hospital order, ss 60, 65
35.	53	arson	PMO/NHSx2	*psychotic* (previous leucotomy)	hospital order, s 60

36.	20	arson (Ms charge dropped)	PMO/SER	(confused/immature/hysterical)	conditional discharge
37.	38	arson	PMO/SER	(anxiety state/battered wife/manipulative/difficult)	probation
38.	40	arson	SER/PMO/NHSx2	*schizophrenia* (cannot cope in community)	hospital order s 60

FEMALE ACQUISITIVE

No.	Age	Charge	Reports	Diagnoses (+ other comments)	Disposal
39.	39	theft	NHS/SER	*depression/agoraphobia* (alcoholic/unstable)	42 days, suspended
40.	20	theft	PMO/SER	*personality disorder* (drug abuse/immature/frighted)	probation
41.	33	robbery	PMO/NHS/SER	(addiction/previous epilepsy/fearful/frail/isolated)	psychiatric probation
42.	33	theft	SER/NHS	(unhappy/addicted/anxious/vulnerable/insecure)	psychiatric probation
43.	24	theft	SER/NHS	(emotionally immature/vulnerable/low IQ)	probation
44.	45	theft	SER/NHS	(unstable family)	fine £50
45.	51	theft	NHS/SER	*depressed* (history of depression)	conditional discharge
46.	28	theft	PMO/SER	(emotionally liable but not ill/depressed/unrealistic	fine £65
47.	21	theft	SER/GP	(single out-of-character offence/family stress/upset)	fine £10

FEMALE PERSONAL VIOLENCE

No.	Age	Charge	Victim	Reports	Diagnoses (+ other comments)	Disposal
48.	55	GBH	adult son	SER/PMOx2/NHS	*depression* (anxious, frightened)	hospital order, s 60
49.	28	assault	friend	NHS/SER	(immature/abnormal personality/difficult/maladjusted)	psychiatric probation (in-patient)
50.	20	wounding	stranger	SER/PMO/NHS	(eating problems/sexual conflicts/?premenstrual/poor self-control)	probation (informal psychiatric treatment)
51.	35	ABH	stranger	NHSx2	*schizophrenia*	hospital order, s 60
52.	25	wounding	stranger	PMO/SER	(lesbian/depressed/lonely)	1 month prison
53.	25	ABH	stranger	private	*addiction* (personality problems)	probation (informal psychiatric treatment)

No.	Age	Charge	Conviction	Victim	Reports	Diagnoses (+ other comments)	Disposal
54.	25	ABH		boyfriend	PMO/SER	(unstable/immature/difficult)	conditional discharge
55.	28	ABH		acquaint.	NHS/SER	severe personality disorder (disturbed)	psychiatric probation
56.	28	assault		stranger	NHS/SER	(isolated)	bound over, £100
57.	26	ABH		acquaint	SER/NHS	anxiety state (family crisis/stress)	probation
58.	30	assault		acquaint	NHS/SER	(treatment with tranquilizers)	fine £30

MALE HOMICIDES

No.	Age	Charge	Conviction	Victim	Reports	Diagnoses (+ other comments)	Disposal
66.	47	murder/arson	as charge	acquaint.	PMO/SER	(tension, depressed)	life prison
67.	36	murder	Ms(P,NI)	acquaint.	NHS/SER	(alcohol and drug abuse)	2 years prison
68.	25	murder	Ms(P,NI)	stranger	SER	(institutionalized/inadequate)	2 years prison
69.	45	murder	Ms(P,NI)	acquaint.	SER	(no pathology mentioned)	2 years prison
70.	18	manslaughter	as charge	stranger	SER/PMO	(unremarkably delinquent)	3 years prison
71.	20	murder/robbery	Ms(NI)/robbery	stranger	SER/PMO	(no pathology mentioned)	7 years prison
72.	21	(as 71)	(as 71)	(as 71)	(as 71)	(as 71)	2 years prison
73.	21	(as 71)	(as 71)	(as 71)R	PMOx2/SER	(delinquent/unusual ideas/ social isolation/maladjusted	7 years prison
74.	44	murder/burglary	Ms(NI) burglary	stranger	PMO	(self-pity/suicide threats)	14 years prison
75.	30	murder/burglary	Ms(NI) burglary	stranger	PMO	PD (brain damaged/heavy drinker/ suicide threats)	14 years prison
76.	35	murder/wounding	Ms(P)	acquaint.	PMO	(no pathology mentioned)	6 years prison
77.	22	murder/robbery	Ms(NI)	landlady	PMO/SER	PD (disturbed/inadequate)	7 years prison
78.	20	murder/robbery	as charged	landlady	PMO/SER	(abnormal relationships/ self mutilation)	life prison
79.	18	murder	Ms(NI)	stranger	SER/PMO	(no pathology mentioned)	4 years prison
80.	28	murder	Ms(DR)	stranger	PMO/NHs/SER	serious psychopath (suicidal)	life prison
81.	41	murder	Ms(DR)	ex-wife	NHS/SERx2/PMO	PD/Dp(insecure/family stress)	4 years prison
82.	38	murder	as charged	friend	PMO	(alcoholic/depressed/psy.hist')	life prison

No.	Age	Charge	Conviction	Victim	Reports	Diagnoses (+ other comments)	Disposal
83.	25	murder	Ms(NI)	acquaint.	PMO/SER	(personality probs/alcoholism/gross functional disturbance)	8 years prison
84.	47	murder	Ms(DR)	ex wife + her lover	NHSx2/PMO	*schizophrenia* (dangerous)	hospital order, ss 60, 65
85.	30	murder	Ms(NI)	wife	PMO	(no pathology noted)	2 years prison

(SUPPLEMENTARY CASES) MALE DOMESTIC HOMICIDES

No.	Age	Charge	Conviction	Victim	Reports	Diagnoses (+ other comments)	Disposal
86.	20	murder	Ms(P)	father	SER/PMO/NHS	(no disorder/excessively timid)	probation
87.	33	murder	Ms(P,NI)	girlfriend	PMO	(no pathology mentioned)	2 years prison
88.	28	murder	as charge	girlfriend	PMO	(low IQ/impulsive)	life prison
89.	30	murder	Ms(DR)	wife	PMO/NHSx2/SER	*paranoid psychosis*	hospital order, ss 60, 65
90.	26	murder	as charge	new bride	PMO/SER	(no pathology noted)	life prison
91.	24	murder	as charge	sister's lover	PMO	(no pathology noted)	life prison
92.	47	murder/arson	as charge	wife	PMO/NHS/Priv	*mental disorder/atypical depressive illness* (suicidal/?psychotic)	life prison
93.	41	murder	Ms(P)	wife	PMO	(tearful/dejected/suicidal)	3 years prison
94.	71	murder	as charge	wife + stepchild	PMOx2	(?pathological jealousy)	life prison
95.	50	murder	Ms(DR)	wife	PMO/NHS	*paranoid psychosis*	hospital order, ss 60, 65
96.	23	murder	Ms(DR)	girlfriend	PMO/NHS	*psychotic*(?malingering/drug abuse)	hospital order, ss 60, 65

MALE ARSON

No.	Age	Charge	Reports	Diagnoses (+ other comments)	Disposal
97.	18	arson	SER/NHSx2	*psychopathic/subnormal* (existing in-patient)	hospital order, s 60
98.	29	c'damage	SER/PMO	(alcohol problems/inadequate/immature)	12 months prison
99.	44	arson	NHS/SER/PMO	*reactive depression/personality disorder* (inadequate/irresponsible/suicide attempts)	2 years prison
100.	24	arson	SER/NHS	*personality disorder* (isolated, suicidal)	probation
101.	25	conspiracy to arson (as 101)	NHSx2/PMOx2	*drug addict/personality disorder* (?psychotic)	1 year prison
102.	24		SER/PMO	(shy/lonely/withdrawn/depressed)	4 months suspended
103.	21	arson	SER/priv/SH	*subnormal/psychopath* (epileptic/immature/suicidal)	hospital order, ss 60, 65
104.	23	arson	NHS/SER/PMO	(drug addiction/tearful/insomnia/withdrawn/alcoholic)	8 years prison
105.	24	arson	SER/NHS	(alcoholic/depressed/seriously suicidal)	probation
106.	28	arson	PMO	(moodswings)	not guilty
107.	31	arson	PMOx2/NHS	*personality disorder* (epileptic/'explosive'/depressed)	7 years prison
108.	29	arson	SER/PMO	(depressed/frustrated/inadequate personality)	2 years prison
109.	35	arson	PMO	*reactive depression*	2 years prison

MALE ACQUISITIVE

No.	Age	Charge	Reports	Diagnoses (+ other comments)	Disposal
110.	21	theft	NHS/SER	(depressed in prison, ?suicidal)	5 months
111.	24	theft	PMO	(no pathology noted)	1 year suspended
112.	24	burglary	SER/NHS	*schizophrenia*	probation
113.	28	theft	PMO/SER	*personality disorder* (drug problems)	9 months prison
114.	27	theft	NHS/SER	*hysterical personality disorder* (psychotic episodes)	[pending]
115.	32	burglary	PMO	(abnormal personality, psychotic symptoms ? ?malingering)	[pending]

No.	Age	Charge	Victim	Reports	Diagnoses (+ other comments)	Disposal
116.	28	burglary		NHS	mental retardation (very high anxiety/depressed)	1 year prison
117.	29	robbery		NHS/PMO/SER	depression/personality disordre (hedonist/alcoholic/tension/anxiety/irresponsible/depressed/?suicidal)	2 years suspended
118.	38	theft		SER/NHS	(psychiatric history)	fine £50
119.	31	burglary		SER/PMO	(odd behaviour in prison/?malingering)	fine £150
120.	22	theft		SER/NHS	epileptic (?psychiatric history)	not guilty

MALE PERSONAL VIOLENCE

No.	Age	Charge	Victim	Reports	Diagnoses (+ other comments)	Disposal
121.	20	assault/GBH/robbery	stranger	PMO	(dangerous)	life prison
122.	22	assault/c'dam age	stranger	SER/PMO	personality disorder (drug problems/impulsive, aggressive)	18 months prison
123.	34	robbery	stranger	PMO	chronic schizophrenia	2 years prison
124.	20	GBH	stranger	PMO	(past history of brain damage + epilepsy)	2 years suspended
125.	24	ABH	stranger	NHSx2/PMO/SER	schizophrenia/psychotic illness	hospital order, s 60
126.	39	assault	stranger	PMO	(past psychiatric history)	18 months suspended
127.	31	ABH/arson	wife	PMOx2	reactive depression/personality disorder (past suicide attempts)	3 years prison
128.	44	ABH	friend	PMO	(no pathology mentioned)	3 months suspended
129.	38	GBH	employer	PMO/SER	(depressed in prison/stress)	community service

Notes to Table 2

1   *Charge/conviction*: These are listed separately for homicide cases, where the conviction was often for a lesser offence than that charged. The following abbreviations are used in these columns:
  ABH: assult occasioning actual bodily harm
  Ars: arson
  Attempt: attempted
  C' damage: criminal damage
  DR: on ground of diminished responsibility
  GBH: assault occasioning grievous bodily harm
  Inf'cide: infanticide
  Ms: manslaughter
  NI: by reason of lack of specific intent to commit murder ('no intent')
  P: by reason of provocation

2   *Reports*: Noted here are all reports included in the court file, or known to have been prepared even though missing from the file. The following abbreviations are used to indicate the authorship of reports;
  GP: general practitioner
  NHS: National Health Service psychiatrist
  PMO: prison medical officer
  Priv/private: privately employed psychiatrist
  SER: (social enquiry report), probation officer
  SH: Special Hospital psychiatrist
  SW: social worker

3   *Diagnoses and other comments*: Any formal diagnoses of current psychiatric disorder appearing in any of the reports are italicized in this column. The material in brackets relates to problems, symptoms or pathologies that are mentioned, but not accorded any specific diagnostic significance. Sometimes these are non-medical problems, (such as 'family difficulties'); at other times they are quasi-medical symptoms, (such as 'depressed mood'), where the author specifies that the symptoms are not sufficient to justify any specific diagnosis. Where several reports are prepared, there are often disagreements in their diagnoses and comments. The inclusion of a diagnosis or problem in this category means only that it was recorded in at least one of the reports; others of the reports may not have shared this conclusion. Any diagnostic category mentioned in a non-medical report (e.g. from social worker) is not recorded as a formal diagnosis, but is included in the bracketed material. Any diagnosis or conclusion about which the authors themselves expressed uncertainty is preceded by a question mark. The following abbreviations are used:
  Dis: disorder
  Dp: depression/depressive disorder

Low IQ: low intelligence not formally diagnosed as mental subnormality or impairment

OD: overdose

PD: personality disorder

Pp: psychopath (ic disorder)

Prob(s): problem(s)

Psy. Hist': past history of psychiatric treatment

Self-harm: history of self-mutilation

4 Disposal: The following abbreviations are used:

prison: immediate imprisonment

s 37: compulsory detention in hospital under section s 37 of the 1983 Mental Health Act

s 60, 65: compulsory detention in hospital under section 60 or 65 of the 1959 Mental Health Act

SSSO: suspended sentence supervision order (i.e. suspended sentence plus supervision by probation officer)

Appendix C

Interviews with professional personnel

The following sets of questions formed the basis of interviews with the various groups of professional personnel. The structure of questions was flexible, and I asked further questions or sought further clarification where it seemed useful to do so. Interviews lasted between half an hour and an hour, and were recorded either in notes or on tape-cassette, depending on the preferences of the interviewee.

Magistrates, lawyers, probation officers

(Introduction to interview questions)
My research is about the whole process whereby particular offenders are identified as mentally abnormal or as needing psychiatric treatment. I'm interested in how these cases are picked out, and what kinds of factors are taken into account. My research covers the whole period from arrest to sentencing, and I'm interested in the contribution of all the different groups involved in this process. The questions I'm going to be asking you are mostly to do with your own involvement in this process, but I'm also interested in your view of the system as a whole. First, I'd like to ask you about the amount of contact that you have with cases of this kind.

1 *In an average month or year, how many cases involving psychiatric factors are you likely to have to deal with? Have you any idea what proportion of your cases that might be?*

2 *And how many of these would be referred to psychiatrists? Can you say anything about the decision to ask for psychiatric assessment? Who is it who usually suggests that a particular defendant should see a psychiatrist?*

3   *Thinking back over the last few cases where psychiatric factors have been involved, can you tell me any of the specific things that made you feel a psychiatric referral might be appropriate?*
- *anything about the defendant/behaviour/circumstances?*
- *any particular groups of defendants?*
- *anything about the offence?*

Can you give me some idea of what a typical case involving psychiatric factors might be like?

4   *When you get a psychiatric report, do you usually find it useful? Are there any common problems with psychiatric reports?*

5   *Can you tell me something about the kinds of cases where some kind of psychiatric disposal might be made? Can you tell me about the last couple of cases of this kind that you've dealt with? Are there any kinds of cases that pose particular problems?*

6   *Apart from cases where a formal psychiatric disposal is made, are there any other cases where psychiatric factors are important for the decision at sentencing?*

7   *We hear a lot in the press about cases where there's disagreement about the involvement of psychiatry in sentencing. In the kinds of cases that you deal with, do you usually find people agree on the proper course to take? Are there any problems?*

Doctors

(General introduction as above)

1   *In an average month or year, how many patients get sent to you through the courts?*

2   *Roughly what proportion of your work consists of doing assessments and reports for the courts?*

3   *How do these cases get referred to you? Are you able to talk to the people making the referral to find out why they think it's necessary? How much information are you normally given about the case?*

4   *Are there any particular kinds of cases that are particularly likely to be referred to you? Do you feel the right kinds of cases get sent to you? Too many? Too few?*

5   *When you're making a psychiatric assessment for the courts, what do you actually* do?
- *interview the defendant? (how long? how often?)*
- *contact anyone else? (GP? Relatives? Other medical staff? Court staff?)*
- *use any past records?*

And what kinds of factors would you be looking out for?
- *in relation to defendant's history and circumstances?*
- *in relation to the offence?*
- *in relation to behaviour and statements in interview?*

6   *Can you tell me something about the kinds of cases where you might recommend a psychiatric disposal, or be willing to offer treatment? Could you perhaps give me some typical examples? Or tell me about the last couple of cases you've seen? What would you see as the treatment for each of these cases?*

7   *Can you tell me about the kinds of cases where you* wouldn't *recommend or offer treatment?*

8   *Does the fact that a patient comes to you from the courts make any difference to these decisions?*

9   *We hear a lot in the press about the cases where there's disagreement about the involvement of psychiatry in sentencing. In the kinds of cases you deal with, do you usually find people agree on the proper course to take? Are there any problems?*

Bibliography and references

Adams, P. and Minson, J. (1978). 'The Subject of Feminism', *m/f*, London, 2, 43.

Al-Issa, I. (1980). *The Psychopathology of Women*, Englewood Cliffs, Prentice Hall.

Allen, H. (1984). 'At the Mercy of Her Hormones: Premenstrual Tension and the Law', *m/f*, London, 9, 19.

Allen, H. (1986). 'Psychiatry and the Construction of the Feminine', in P. Miller and N. Rose (eds), *The Power of Psychiatry*, Cambridge, Polity Press.

Anderson, E. (1976). 'The "Chivalrous" Treatment of the Female Offender in the Arms of the Criminal Justice System: A Review of the Literature', *Social Problems*, Buffalo, New York, 3, 23, 349.

Armstrong, G. (1977). 'Females Under the Law – "Protected" but Unequal', *Crime & Deliquency*, San Francisco, 23, 2 109.

Bottoms, A. and McWilliams, W. (1979). 'A Non-Treatment Paradigm for Probation Practice', *Brit J Social Work*, London, 9, 2 159.

Bowden, P. (1978). 'Men Remanded into Custody for Medical Reports: the Selection for Treatment', *British Journal of Psychiatry*, London, 132, 320.

Bowker, L. (ed). (1978). *Women, Crime and the Criminal Justice System*, Massachusetts, USA, Heath & Co.

Brewer, C., Morris, T., Morgan, P. and North, M. (1981). *Criminal Welfare on Trial*, London, Social Affairs Unit.

Brewer, C. (1981). 'Compulsory Therapy for Crime: Bad Habits are not Diseases', in Brewer *et al.*, *Criminal Welfare on Trial*, London, Social Affairs Unit.

Broverman, I., Broverman, D., Clarkson, F., Rosenkrantz, P. and Vogel, S. (1970). 'Sex Role Stereotypes and Mental Health', *Journal of Consulting and Clinical Psychology*, Washington D. C., 34, 1f.

Busfield, J. (1983). 'Gender, Mental Illness and Psychiatry', in M. Evans and C. Ungerson, (eds), *Sexual Divisions, Patterns and Processes*, London, Tavistock.

Butler, Lord (Chairman). (1975). *Report of the Committee on Mentally Abnormal Offenders*, London, HMSO.

Carlen, P. (1983). *Women's Imprisonment: A Study in Social Control*, London, Routledge & Kegan Paul.

Carlen, P. (1986). A Psychiatry in Prisons: Promises, Premises, Practices and Politics', in P. Miller and N. Rose (eds), *The Power of Psychiatry*, Cambridge, Polity Press.

Carlen, P. and Collinson, M. (1980). *Radical Issues in Criminology*, Oxford, Martin Robertson.

Cheedle, J. and Ditchfield, J. (1982). *Sentenced Mentally Ill Offenders*, London, Home Office Research and Planning Unit.

Chesler, P. (1974). *Women and Madness*, London, Allen Lane.

Chesney-Lind, M. (1977). 'Judicial Paternalism and the Female Status Offender: Training Women to Know Their Place', *Crime and Deliquency*, San Francisco, 23, 121.

Chesney-Lind, M. (1978). 'Chivalry Re-examined: Women and the Criminal Justice System', in L. Bowker (ed), *Women, Crime and the Criminal Justice System*, Massuchusetts, USA, Heath and Co.

Chiswick, D., McIsaac, M. and McLintock, F. (1984). *Prosecution of Mentally Disturbed Offenders: Dilemmas of Identification and Discretion*, Aberdeen, Aberdeen University Press.

Clare, A. (1976). *Psychiatry in Dissent*, London, Tavistock.

Cohen, S. and Taylor, L. (1976). *Prison Secrets*, London, Pluto Press.

Coid, J. (1984). 'How Many Psychiatric Patients in Prison?', *British Journal of Psychiatry*, London, 145, 78.

Conrad, P. and Schneider, J. (1980). *Deviance and Medicalisation: from Badness to Sickness*, London, Mosby.

Cousins, M. (1980). 'Men's Rea: A Note on Sexual Difference, Criminology and the Law', in P. Carlen and M. Collinson (eds), *Radical Issues in Criminology*, Oxford, Martin Robertson.

Cowie, J., Cowie, V., and Slater, E. (1968). *Delinquency in Girls*, London, Heinemann.

Craft, M. (1984). 'Should One Treat or Gaol Psychopaths?' in A. Craft and M. Craft (eds), *Mentally Abnormal Offenders*, Eastbourne, Bailliere-Tindall.

Craft, A. and Craft, M. (eds), (1984). *Mentally Abnormal Offenders*, Eastbourne, Bailliere-Tindall.

Cross, R. (1981). *The English Sentencing System*, London, Butterworths.

Cross, R. and Jones, P. (1980). *Introduction to Criminal Law*, London, Butterworths.

Crown, S. (ed). (1981). *Practical Psychiatry, vol. 1*, London, Northwood.

Curran, D. (1983). 'Judicial Discretion and Defendant's Sex', *Criminology*, Columbus OH, 21, 1–Feb, 41.

Datesman, S. and Scarpitti, F. (1980). *Women, Crime and Justice*, Oxford, Oxford University Press.

DeCrow, K. (1974). *Sexist Justice*, New York, Random House.

Dell, S. and Gibbens, T. (1971). 'Remands of Women Offenders for Medical Reports', *Medicine, Science and the Law*, Brentford, Middlesex, 11, 117.

Department of Health and Social Security. (1981). *Care in the Community*, London, HMSO.

Department of Health and Social Security. (1986). Mental Health Statistics for England (annual publication), London, HMSO.

Devlin, Lord. (1963). in R. MacDonald (ed), *Changing Legal Objectives*, Toronto, Toronto University Press.

Dohrenwend, B. and Dohrenwend, B. (1976). 'Sex Differences and Psychiatric Disorders', *American Journal of Sociology*, Chicago, 6, 1447.

D'Orban, P. (1971). 'Social and Psychiatric Aspects of Female Crime', *Medicine, Science and the Law*, Brentford, Middlesex, 11, 104.

Dove-Wilson, Sir J. (Chairman). (1932). *Report of the Departmental Committee on Persistent Offenders*, London, HMSO.

East, N. and Hubert, W. (Chairmen). (1939). *Report on the Psychological Treatment of Crime*, London, HMSO.

Eaton, M. (1983). 'Mitigating Circumstances: Familiar Rhetoric', *International Journal of the Sociology of Law*, London. 1983, 11, 385.

Edwards, S. (1981). *Female Sexuality and the Law; a Study of Constructs of Femininity as They Inform Statute and Legal Procedure*, Oxford, Robertson.

Edwards, S. (1984). *Women on Trial*, Manchester, Manchester University Press.

Edwards, S. (1985). *Gender, Sex and the Law*, London, Croom Helm.

Evans, M. and Ungerson, C. (eds). (1983). *Sexual Divisions, Patterns and Processes*, London, Tavistock.

Farrington, D. and Morris, A. (1983). 'Do Magistrates Discriminate Against Men?', *Justice of the Peace*, Chichester, 147/38, 601.

Faulk, M. (1976). 'A Psychiatric Study of Men Serving a Sentence in Winchester Prison', *Medicine Science and the Law*, Brentford, Middlexex, 16, 244.

Floud, J. and Young, W. (1981). *Dangerousness and Criminal Justice*, London, Heinemann.

Foucault, M. (1967). *Madness and Civilization*. (trans. Richard Howard), London, Tavistock.

Foucault, M. (1972). *The archaeology of Knowledge*, (trans. Alan Sheridan), London, Tavistock.

Foucault, M. (1977). *Discipline and Punish*. (trans. Alan Sheridan), London, Tavistock.

Gibbens, T. (1981). Preparing Court Reports, in Crown, S. (ed), *Practical Psychiatry, vol. 1*, London, Northwood.

Gibbens, T., Soothill, K. and Pope, P. (1977). *Medical Remands in the Criminal Court*, Maudsley Monograph, no. 25, Oxford, Oxford University Press.

Gibbens, T., Soothill, K., and Way, C. (1981). 'Psychiatric Treatment on Probation', *British Journal of Criminology*, London, 21, 324.

Gostin, L. (1983). *A Practical Guide to Mental Health Law*, London, MIND.

Gunn, J., Roberton, G., Dell, S., Way, C. and Maxwell, E. (1978). *Psychiatric Aspects of Imprisonment*, London, Academic Press.

Hansard. (Weekly Bulletin of the Proceedings of the House of Commons), London, HMSO.

Harris, B. (1979). 'Rehabilitation – After the Fall', *Law Society's Gazette*, London, 14.10.79.

Harris, G. (1981). *Essex Police Community Services Branch*, (Internal document), Essex Police Force.

Haxby, D. (1978). *Probation: A Changing Service*, London, Constable.

Higgins, J. (1984). 'The Regional Secure Unit', in Craft, A. and Craft, M. (eds), *Mentally Abnormal Offenders*, Eastbourne, Bailliere-Tindall.

Hines, V. (1982). *Judicial Discretion in Sentencing by Judges and Magistrates*, Chichester, Rose.

Hirst, P. and Woolley, P. (1982). *Social Relations and Human Attributes*, London, Tavistock.

Home Office. (annual). *Criminal Statistics for England and Wales*, London, HMSO.

Home Office. (annual). *Report of the Work of the Prison Service*, London, HMSO.

Home Office. (annual). *Prison Statistics*, London, HMSO.

Home Office. (1959). *Penal Practice in a Changing Society*, Home Office White Paper, London, HMSO.

Home Office. (1969). *People in Prison, England and Wales*, London, HMSO.

Home Office. (1977). *Prisons and the Prisoner*, London, HMSO.

Home Office. (1978). *The Sentence of the Court*, London, HMSO.

Jones, K. (1972). *A History of the Mental Health Services*, London, Routledge & Kegan Paul.

The Justices' Clerks' Society. (1982). *Observations on the Mental Health (Amendment) Bill*, (PO Box 107, Bristol BS99 7BJ).

Klein, D. (1980). 'The Etiology of Female Crime: a Review of the Literature', in S. Datesman and F. Scarpitti (eds), *Women, Crime and Justice*, Oxford, Oxford University Press.

Konopka, G. (1966). *The Adolescent Girl in Conflict*, New Jersey, Englewood Cliffs.

Kruttschnitt, C. (1982). 'Women, Crime and Dependency', *Criminology*, Columbus OH, 19/4, 495.

Law Commission. (1977). *Report on Defences of General Application*, London, HMSO.

Law Commission. (1978). *Report on the Mental Element in Crime*, London, HMSO.

Lawson, A. (1966). *The Recognition of Mental Illness in London*, Maudsley Monograph no. 15, Oxford, Oxford University Press.

Lawson, W. (1984). 'Mentally Abnormal Offenders in Prison', in Craft, A. and Craft, M. (eds), *Mentally Abnormal Offenders*, Eastbourne, Bailliere-Tindall.

Lewis, P. (1980). *Psychiatric Probation Orders, Roles and Expectations of Probation Officers and Psychiatrists*, Cambridge, Cambridge Institute of Criminology.

Loucas, K. (1980). 'Broadmoor's Relationship with the National Health Service Psychiatric Hospitals', *Bulletin of the Royal College of Psychiatrists*, London, 133.

Macdonald, R. (ed). (1963). *Changing Legal Objectives*, Toronto, Toronto University Press.

May, J. (Chairman). (1979). *Report on the Committee of Enquiry into the UK Prison Services*, London, HMSO.

Mayer-Gross, W., Slater, E., and Roth, M. (1960). *Clinical Psychiatry*, London, Cassel and Co.

Menniger, K. (1968). *The Crime of Punishment*, Harmondsworth, Penguin.

Miller, P. and Rose, N. (1986). *The Power of Psychiatry*, Cambridge, Polity Press.

Moran, R. (1982). *Knowing Right from Wrong: The Insanity Defence of Daniel McNaughten*, New York, Free Press.

Moulds, E. (1980). 'Chivalry and Paternalism in the Criminal Justice System', in S. Datesman and F. Scarpitti (eds), *Women, Crime and Justice*, Oxford, Oxford University Press.

Orr, J. (1978). 'The Imprisonment of Mentally Disordered Offenders', *British Journal of Psychiatry*, London, 133, 191.

Pailthorpe, G. (1932(1)). *What We Put in Prison and in Preventive Rescue Homes*, London, Williams & Norgate.

Pailthorpe, G. (1932(2)). *Studies in the Psychology of Delinquency*, Medical Research Council Special Report no. 170, London, HMSO.

Parsons, T. (1950). 'Illness and the Role of the Physician', *American Journal of Orthopsychiatry*, New York, 21, 452.

Parsons, T. (1951). *The Social System*, London, Routledge & Kegan Paul.

Parton, N. (1985). *The Politics of Child Abuse*, London, Macmillan.

Pollak, O. (1950). *The Criminality of Women*, Pennsylvania, University of Pennsylvania Press.

Ramon, S. (1986). 'The Category of Psychopathy: its Professional and Social Context in Britain', in Miller, P. and Rose, N. (eds), *The Power of Psychiatry*, Cambridge, Polity Press.

Rose, N. (1985). *The Psychological Complex: Psychology, Politics and Society in England, 1869–1939*, London, Routledge & Kegan Paul.

Rose, N. (1986). 'The Discipline of Mental Health', in P. Miller and N. Rose (eds), *The Power Of Psychiatry*, Cambridge, Polity Press.

Sachs, A. and Hoff-Wilson, J. (1978). *Sexism and The Law*, London, Martin Robinson.

Salem, S. (1983). 'Psychiatric Remands: The Courts' Perspective and Alternative Models', *Home Office Research & Planning Bulletin*, London, 16, 32.

Scull, A. (1977). *Decarceration, Community Treatment and the Deviant: A Radical View*, Englewood Cliffs, Prentice Hall.

Scull, A. (1979). *Museums of Madness: The Social Organisation of Insanity in 19th Century England*, London, Allen Lane.

Shapland, J. (1981). *Between Conviction and Sentence*, London, Routledge & Kegan Paul.

Smart, C. (1976). *Women, Crime and Criminology: A Feminist Critique*, London, Routledge & Kegan Paul.

Smith, J. and Hogan, B. (1978). *Criminal Law, 4th edn.*, London, Butterworths.

Smith, R. (1981). *Trial by Medicine: Insanity and Responsibility in Victorian Trials*, Edinburgh, Edinburgh University Press.

Stewart (Lord). (1983). *Keeping Offenders Out of Court: Further Alternatives to Prosecution*, Scottish Home and Health Department and Crown Office, Edinburgh, HMSO.

Thomas, D. (1979). *Principles of Sentencing*, 2nd edn., London, Heinemann.

Trick, K. and Tennent, T. (1981). *Forensic Psychiatry*, London, Pinman.

Walker, N. (1968). *Crime and Insanity In England, vol. 1*, Edinburgh, Edinburgh University Press.

Walker, N. and McCabe, S. (1973). *Crime and Insanity In England, vol. 2*, Edinburgh, Edinburgh University Press.

Wallace, M. (1986) *The Silent Twins*, Englewood Cliffs, Prentice-Hull.

Williams, G. (1978). *Textbook of Criminal Law*, London, Stephens and Sons.

Wootton, Baroness. (1960). 'Diminished Responsibility: a Layman's View', *Law Quarterly Review*, London, 224.

Index

[*Note*: italicized entries refer to legal cases]